Beginner's CHINESE *script*

Elizabeth Scurfield and Song Lianyi

TEACH YOURSELF BOOKS

√RAP 445-1045

For UK orders: please contact Bookpoint Ltd, 78 Milton Park, Abingdon, Oxon
OX14 4TD. Telephone: (44) 01235 400414, Fax: (44) 01235 400454. Lines are open
from 9.00–6.00, Monday to Saturday, with a 24 hour message answering service.
Email address: orders@bookpoint.co.uk

For U.S.A. & Canada orders: please contact NTC/Contemporary Publishing, 4255
West Touhy Avenue, Lincolnwood, Illinois 60646–1975, U.S.A. Telephone:
(847) 679 5500, Fax: (847) 679 2494.

Long renowned as the authoritative source for self-guided learning – with more than
30 million copies sold worldwide – the Teach Yourself series includes over 200 titles in
the fields of languages, crafts, hobbies, business and education.

British Library Cataloguing in Publication Data
A catalogue record for this title is available from The British Library.

Library of Congress Catalog Card Number: On file.

First published in UK 1999 by Hodder Headline Plc, 338 Euston Road, London, NW1 3BH.

First published in US 1999 by NTC/Contemporary Publishing, 4255 West Touhy Avenue,
Lincolnwood (Chicago), Illinois 60646–1975 U.S.A.

The 'Teach Yourself' name and logo are registered trade marks of Hodder & Stoughton Ltd.

Typeset by Graphicraft Limited, Hong Kong.
Printed in Great Britain for Hodder & Stoughton Educational, a division of Hodder
Headline Plc, 338 Euston Road, London NW1 3BH by Cox & Wyman Ltd, Reading,
Berkshire.

Impression number   10 9 8 7 6 5 4 3 2 1
Year   2005 2004 2003 2002 2001 2000 1999

Dedications

To my partner, Martina Weitsch, who has pilot-tested the exercises in this book and made a host of helpful suggestions.

To Kelin, my daughter, who has inspired me throughout the production of this book.

Acknowledgements

We would like to thank Lu Wenzhu for her contribution to the artwork and Zhao Yizhou for his calligraphy. Last, but not least, we would like to thank Sue Hart and Carolyn Taylor for their invaluable support and encouragement.

Bibliographical details

Elizabeth Scurfield graduated with a First Class honours degree in Chinese from the School of Oriental and African Studies in London. She has over 26 years' experience of teaching Chinese to beginners successfully. She is currently Director of Marketing and Admissions and Head of Chinese at the University of Westminster.

Song Lianyi grew up and was educated in Beijing. He has taught Chinese as a foreign language for ten years, seven of these in the UK. He is currently lecturer in Chinese at the School of Oriental and African Studies, University of London. He has a PhD in language education awarded by the University of London.

CONTENTS

INTRODUCTION

Most people take one look at the Chinese script and say 'Oh no, I couldn't possibly learn that, it's much too complicated' or perhaps 'I'm no good at drawing so I wouldn't be able to write Chinese'. By the time you get to the end of this book you will have realised that neither of these statements is true. You may decide that you have not got the *time* to learn the Chinese script but that is a different matter. Anybody of average intelligence and with a reasonable visual memory who is prepared to put in the necessary time *can* master the Chinese script.

The Chinese script is an amazing tool with which you will be able to go some way towards understanding Chinese, one of the world's most ancient languages, and its culture.

Teach Yourself Beginner's Chinese Script starts from scratch, explaining the origins of the language and how characters have evolved. It teaches you how to write characters correctly from the beginning and, through a series of carefully graded exercises, how to understand enough from signs, directions, instructions and even menus to be able to get by. You will surprise yourself with your ingenuity and your ability to guess correctly, based on the sound logic learnt from this book.

This book is to be enjoyed, with many examples taken from real life. By the time you have finished it, we hope you will have caught the Chinese bug – hours of enjoyment (and hard work) lie ahead of you!

How to use the book

The book is divided into two main parts. Units 1–4 introduce you to the origins of the Chinese script, explain how characters and words are formed and the basic rules in writing them. Unit 4 ends with a mini-test to enable you to check your progress so far.

Units 5–9 introduce you to real-life situations such as reading signs, maps, notices and even menus. You will be able to write numbers, dates, tell the time and fill out simple forms. There is a comprehensive test at the end of Unit 9.

Unit 10 explains how to use a Chinese–English dictionary and Chinese word-processing packages with concrete examples. There is also a brief introduction to Chinese idioms.

At the back of the book

At the back of the book there is a reference section which contains:

a key to the exercises
a table of radicals for easy reference
a guide to pronunciation and tones
useful public signs and notices
a Chinese–English vocabulary list containing all the characters in the course, listed according to radical and with the number of the unit where they first occurred
an English–Chinese vocabulary list containing all the most important words which have occurred in the course

UNIT 1
Origins of the script

Many ancient peoples wrote in symbols, including the Chinese. The most well known are perhaps Egyptian hieroglyphics carved on stone or written on papyrus. What was common to all the known ancient scripts was that at their earliest form of development they consisted of picture signs, many of which looked quite similar.

Chinese									
Hittite									
Egyptian									
Sumerian									

The differences, however, are also striking. Look at two of the signs for water for instance (third row from right). The Egyptian sign seems to represent calm water, whereas the Chinese sign indicates a winding river flooding its banks, which is just what the Yellow River (known as the cradle of Chinese civilisation) used to do.

We still use symbols or signs today as a kind of international language which overcomes communication barriers on a very basic but necessary level.

Exercise 1

What do the following signs mean?

a) _____   b) _____   c) _____   d) _____

e) _____   f) _____   g) _____

The earliest examples of written Chinese are found on the oracle bones
used in divination rites in the Shang dynasty (c1500BC–1066BC). Nearly
2,500 separate characters have been found on bone fragments dating back
to this period, so the total in use must have been much greater than this.
Of these characters, approximately 600 have been identified.

These are characters appearing on oracle bones. They are very different
from the writing of today.

The first step in building up a written language in China was the use of
pictured objects or pictographs to represent the objects themselves. About
10% of all characters in modern Chinese come from these pictographs.

Here are a few examples of pictographs showing the evolution of some characters into their present form. The earliest form of the character is on the left, the one used today is on the extreme right.

⊙	⊖	⊟	日	*rì*	sun
☽	☽	☽	月	*yuè*	moon
𓀀	𐦙	𐦚	人	*rén*	person
⍟	⍟	⍟	木	*mù*	tree

☑ Exercise 2

Match up the pictured objects in column 1 with the old forms of the pictogram in columns 2 and 3 and the modern-day form in column 4 (simplified characters in brackets). Write the numbers in the space provided in the last column, for example: *1A 2B 3C 4D*. Then check your answers in the Key to the exercises on page 114.

	1	2	3	4	
A				車(车)	_ _ _ _ _ _ 4A
B				馬(马)	_ _ _ _ _ _ 4B
C				魚(鱼)	_ _ _ _ _ _ 4C
D				雨	_ _ _ _ _ _ 4D
E				山	_ _ _ _ _ _ 4E
F				子	_ _ _ _ _ _ 4F

Why did the ancient Chinese writing system survive but not that of the Egyptians, Hittites or Sumerians? One of the major reasons must be that China was unified at a very early stage in history by the first Qin emperor, Qin Shi Huangdi, in 221BC and unlike the Roman Empire, for example, has stayed unified until the present day. Qin Shi Huangdi also unified the Chinese script. As some of you may know, Chinese has many different spoken forms or dialects, but they are all written in exactly the same way, so all literate Chinese can read the same newspapers and the same books. Japan sent students to study in China as early as the Tang dynasty (618–907AD), so that when the Japanese started to keep written records they 'borrowed' Chinese characters which are still in use in modern written Japanese and are referred to as *kanji*. The Koreans did the same thing although modern Korean contains no Chinese characters.

☑ Exercise 3

See if you can still remember what the characters below mean. Don't worry if you can't remember them all; you can always check your answers in the Key to the exercises at the back of the book.

1. 月   2. 木   3. 山   4. 雨   5. 日
6. 鱼   7. 马   8. 车   9. 子   10. 人

2 | UNIT 2
How Chinese characters
are formed

In Unit 1, we saw how characters evolved from drawings of objects to what they look like today. Drawings, however vivid they might be, are not sufficient to express more complex concepts and ideas, especially more abstract ones. Over the years, these pictographs were extended or combined to form ideographs. Two people on top of the character for earth meant 'to sit' 坐; a woman 女 with a child 子 beside her meant 'good' 好; a pig 豕 under a roof 宀 meant 'home' 家, etc.

Try the following exercise and see if you can work out what these ancient ideographs are trying to express.

Exercise 1

Write out the meaning of the following characters or ideographs. The components of each character are presented with their meaning. You have already seen some of the components in Unit 1. Most of them are meaningful characters in their own right.

					Meaning
囚	人	person	口	enclosure	_____
明	日	sun	月	moon	_____
坐	人	person	土	earth	_____
休	人*	person	木	tree	_____
男	田	field	力	strength	_____

* In combination 人 becomes 亻 on the left-hand side.

Now let's see if you have understood them correctly. A person in an enclosure is a prisoner. Sun and moon together means bright. And as we just saw, two people 'down to earth' means to sit. When a person is against a tree, s/he is 'resting'. The strength in the field comes from a 'man' or a 'male'. Do these make sense to you?

The following characters are composed in the same way as those in Exercise 1. Let's see if you can work out their meanings. Remember these characters were made a long time ago. The concepts in those days might not always be the same as we perceive them today. For instance, why is it 'good' to have a child? Because in traditional Chinese society, as in many others around the world, a child, and more particularly a male child, was necessary to carry on the family line and to worship the ancestors. Children were (and are) also necessary to work in the fields, particularly in the labour-intensive paddy fields.

☑ Exercise 2

Write out the meaning of the following characters in the space provided.

Meaning

信	亻	person	言	speech/words	_____
鲜	鱼	fish	羊	sheep	_____
安	宀	roof	女	woman	_____

A person's words convey a 'message' or can be passed on in writing as a 'letter'. Fish and sheep's meat must be eaten when they are 'fresh'. Once there is a woman in a household, there will be a family which brings 'stability', hence the meaning of 'safe' and 'secure'.

Did you get any of them right? If you did, well done! If you didn't, it's not surprising at this stage. These meanings may be very obscure to the beginner but they tell us a lot about traditional Chinese values such as the importance of the family and of having a male heir.

Word building was not just a matter of putting two pictographs together. This method would still not have created enough new characters to convey many of the ideas and concepts which exist in a developed language. Another method of creating new characters which dated after the Shang dynasty (c1500–1066BC) is sometimes called the phonograph. It is made up of two components, one of which is usually known as the **radical** and the other the **phonetic** which gives a clue as to the character's pronunciation.

What is a radical?

A radical is a component of a character. It sometimes gives us a partial idea of the meaning of the whole character. Just as the Greek prefix 'phil' tells us that the word has something to do with 'love' (*phil*anthropy is the love of humankind, a *phil*osopher is a lover of wisdom etc.), when a

Chinese sees a character with the heart radical written 心 or 忄, depending on its position, s/he can assume that the character has something to do with the emotions. For example, 愛 means 'love; to love', 恨 means 'hate; to hate', 怕 means 'to fear'.

Each character has at least one radical. Some characters are built up of radicals only, but in these cases, one or more of the radicals is acting as the phonetic in that particular character. Let's look at the character 想 *xiǎng* which means 'to miss' or 'think of' (a person or thing) or just 'to think'. It is made up of the heart radical 心 and two other radicals 木 tree and 目 eye, but in this case, when 木 and 目 are put together 相, they are pronounced *xiāng* and they provide the phonetic component for the character 想. Another example is the character 江 *jiāng*, 'river', which is made up of the water radical 氵 and the radical *gōng* 工, meaning 'work'. From the meaning of the character, 'river', 工 is obviously the phonetic element here although it is not particularly helpful as the sound has changed so much. As you can see from all of this, radicals are *not* equivalent to letters in English. All radicals mean something in themselves, but this does not always help with the meaning of the character as a whole. For instance, the fact that the radical for a particular character is a dot 丶 or a horizontal or vertical line 一、丨 helps us to find it in the dictionary but gives us no indication of the meaning of the character whatsoever.

Here is a table of some single or two stroke radicals which do not necessarily carry any meaning. The ones with meaning that you have met so far are listed in a table at the end of this unit. Refer to the radical table at the end of the book for a fuller list.

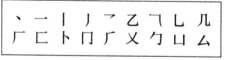

There are around 190–230 radicals in Chinese writing. The discrepancy in numbers results from how some of the radicals are grouped and the inclusion or exclusion of some of the complicated ones. At the beginning of a Chinese dictionary there is usually an index of radicals. The characters in the dictionary are based on the index. In Unit 10 we will show you how to look up a character in a Chinese dictionary.

How are characters formed?

There are a number of ways in which characters are formed. The examples in Exercises 1 and 2 represent one of the most common ways: combining the meanings of two radicals to form a new meaning. The following are some more examples of this.

Radical + radical

竹* (bamboo) + 毛 (fur/hair) = 笔 (Chinese writing brush)
言* (speech) + 舌 (tongue) = 话 (words, speech; to speak)
小 (small)   + 大 (big)   = 尖 (sharp, pointed)
日 (sun)   + 月 (moon)   = 明 (bright)

* Note that 言 becomes 讠 when acting as the radical on the left-hand side of a simplified character, and 竹 becomes ⺮ when acting as the radical on top of a character.

As you may have observed, the position of a radical in a character varies. It can be on the left or right side of a character, or it can be on the top or bottom of a character. It can also be on the inside or outside of a character. It is important to know where a particular radical occurs in a character so that you can identify it and be able to look it up in the dictionary (more on this later). The radical's actual position normally has no bearing on the meaning or interpretation of the character.

竹 bamboo, for instance, always occurs on the top of a character when it looks like ⺮, as does 草 grass, when it looks like ⺿. Fire 火 can occur on the left-hand side of a character as 火 or on the bottom of a character when it looks like ⺣. The radical for speech 言 appears on the left-hand side of a character and is written as 讠 when it is simplified.

☑ Exercise 3

You know 人 means 'person', 木 means 'tree' and 火 means 'fire'. What do you think the following characters mean?

Radicals	Character(s)	Meaning
人 + 人	= 从	_____
人 + 人 + 人	= 众*	_____
木 + 木	= 林	_____
木 + 木 + 木	= 森	_____
火 + 火	= 炎	_____
火 + 火 + 火	= 焱	_____

* This is a simplified character. The principle of making characters, however, remains the same.

In some combinations, as in Exercise 3, the meaning is very clear to the Westerner (at least after it has been given!), but in others it remains very obscure. It is important to be aware that there is not a consistent logic inherent in the formation of all Chinese characters, so that although we can see in some of today's characters how they have developed from their earliest forms, there is no methodology which will serve us for them all. In addition, concepts have changed. Pigs 豕 are rarely kept under the same roof as their owners, but 家 'pig under a roof' still means 'home', villages are seldom made of wood these days, but the character for village 村 still has 木 wood as its radical.

You may well ask: But how do we know how to pronounce these characters? The answer is we don't, at least not for sure in most cases. Unlike languages with an alphabet, Chinese characters do not directly indicate the pronunciation. However, you will find a brief guide to pronunciation at the back of the book starting on page 129.

Radical + phonetic

We have already looked at how the Chinese expanded their written vocabulary by putting two pictograms or two radicals together. The next most common method is what we may call the radical + phonetic method or phonogram which we referred to earlier. The following examples are composed of two parts: a radical conveying meaning and a phonetic element. Although when standing alone, these phonetic elements carry meaning and may or may not be radicals, here they perform the function of indicating the sound to some extent. In the examples which follow, the phonetic or sound element *does* indicate the sound of the whole character, but this is the exception rather the rule. In most cases, characters with the same phonetic element are pronounced slightly differently and mostly in a different tone. (There are four tones in Modern Standard Chinese or Mandarin, seven in Cantonese. Our point of reference in this book is Modern Standard Chinese which is understood by about 70% of the Chinese population.)

You may notice in the following examples, that the characters for 'far' and 'garden' share the same phonetic component. They do sound similar, although one is in the second tone indicated by ´ and the other is in the third tone indicated by ˇ. Characters 'to accompany' and 'to blend' also share the same sound radical and they are pronounced exactly the same, with the same tone, in this case fourth ˋ.

	Sound	Meaning	(Meaning) radical	Sound
远	yuǎn	far	辶 (to walk quickly)	元 (yuán)
碗	wǎn	bowl	石 (stone, mineral)	宛 (wǎn)
们	men*	persons	人 (person)	门 (mén)
伴	bàn	to accompany	人 (person)	半 (bàn)
订	dìng	to book	言 (speech)	丁 (dīng)
钉	dīng	nail	钅 (metal)	丁 (dīng)
锈	xiù	rusty	钅 (metal)	秀 (xiù)
园	yuán	garden	口 (enclosure)	元 (yuán)
房	fáng	house	户 (household)	方 (fāng)
骑	qí*	to ride (a horse)	马 (horse)	奇 (qí)
拌	bàn	to blend	扌 (hand)	半 (bàn)

* Check the pronunciation at the back of the book. It is *not* the same as in English.

By looking at the position of the radicals in the examples in this section and in characters or references earlier in the unit, you should be able to do the next two exercises.

✔ Exercise 4

In each of the characters that follow, the radical is missing. Where does it go? On the top, on the bottom, on the left-hand side or on the right-hand side?

Radicals

1 马 (horse)   累 (mule)   户 (donkey)   句 (pony)
2 艹 (grass)   化 (flower)   早 (grass)   牙 (sprouts)
3 钅 (metal)   冈 (steel)   秀 (rusty)   令 (bell)
4 辶 (to walk)   兆 (escape)   寸 (to pass)   万 (to step over)

✔ Exercise 5

Which character is right? Circle the correct one.

1 to hit   仃 打 订   3 to scorn   饥 机 讥
2 stove   灶 杜 吐   4 snow   雪 扫 灵

Let's summarise the radicals you have seen in these first two units. More radicals will be introduced in Units 3–5. A complete table of radicals will be found in the reference section at the back of the book.

车	vehicle	鱼	fish	木	tree	水 氵	water
宀	roof	大	big	毛	hair, fur	人 亻	person
雨	rain	子	child	土	earth	心 忄	heart
田	field	力	strength	羊	sheep	言 讠	speech
石	stone	日	sun	女	woman	草 艹	grass
辶	walk (quickly)	月	moon	小	small	火 灬	fire
豕	pig	舌	tongue	马	horse	竹 ⺮	bamboo
户	household	口	enclosure	工	work	手 扌	hand
山	mountain					金 钅	metal

✔ Exercise 6

Can you recognise the character according to the following description? Please give what you think is the meaning of each character. We have done one for you.

1 an eye with water   林 _____
2 two trees next to each other   灾 _____
3 bamboo with fur/hair underneath   囚 _____
4 a person in an enclosure   从 to follow ____
5 fire under roof   泪 _____
6 two people next to each other   笔 _____

✔ Exercise 7

Can you identify the meaning of the following characters with the help of their radicals? Again, we have done one for you. Refer back to the table of radicals to help you.

墙   to throw   吻   she
扔   wall   椅   warm
怕   sweat   暖   kiss
汗   fear   她   chair

3 | UNIT 3 *Writing Chinese characters*

Now it's your turn to write Chinese characters! Where do we begin? As you can imagine, there are some basic rules for writing Chinese characters which you need to master. This is important if you are to remember them accurately. Chinese characters should always be written the same way so that they become fixed in your memory. We have seen how most characters are made up of two or more components or structural parts, although some of these components such as 月 *yuè* (moon), 日 *rì* (sun) can stand by themselves as we have mentioned earlier. Although the total number of characters is quite large, the number of components which go to make up these characters is very limited. These components are written with a number of basic strokes, which are illustrated as follows.

Stroke	Name	
`	*diǎn*	dot
—	*héng*	horizontal
│	*shù*	vertical
╱	*piě*	left-falling
╲	*nà*	right-falling
╱	*tí*	rising
ﮑﺍﺍﺍ	*gōu*	hook
﹁﹄	*zhé*	turning

These strokes are basically straight lines and were traditionally written in ink with a hair brush. The main directions are from top to bottom and from left to right. The arrows on the basic strokes that follow show how the characters are written by indicating the direction each stroke takes.

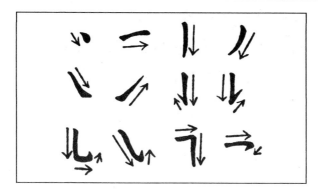

The rules of stroke order in writing Chinese characters and character components are as follows.

Example	Stroke Order						Rule
十	一					十	First horizontal, then vertical
人	丿					人	First left-falling, then right-falling
三	一	二				三	From top to bottom
州	丶	丿	丬	州	州	州	From left to right
月	丿	刀	月			月	First outside, then inside
四	丨	冂	冈	四		四	Finish inside, then close
小	亅	小				小	Middle, then the two sides

Let's go back to the table of radicals in Unit 2 and identify some of these basic strokes. Take the radical 工 for instance; it is made up of two horizontal and one vertical strokes and the rule is first horizontal, then vertical and from top to bottom, so it is written:

一 丁 工

NB. Horizontal strokes must always be written from left to right, viz ⇒. 小 is a symmetrical character so the middle stroke is done first, then the two sides, from left to right:

亅 小 小

土 first horizontal, then vertical and from top to bottom:

一 十 土

口 is an interesting case. When writing what amounts to a box, this part of the box ㄱ is done in one stroke, but this part └ is done as two strokes. This is all to do with what is and is not possible to do with a hair brush without dripping and what looks aesthetically pleasing. So, 口 is written:

丨 冂 口

It is still basically following the rules top to bottom, and from left to right.

目 is very similar in its stroke order but also follows the finish inside, then close rule:

丨 冂 日 目

月 follows the first outside, then inside rule:

丿 刀 月 月

☑ **Exercise 1**

Try working out the stroke order of the following eight characters and writing them in the gaps provided. (The number of gaps indicates the number of strokes required.) Writing small characters needs a lot of practice so we recommend that initially you use a separate sheet for this and subsequent exercises.

1 人 ___ 人
2 田 ___ ___ ___ ___ 田
3 大 ___ ___ 大
4 木 ___ ___ ___ 木
5 钅 ___ ___ ___ 钅
6 山 ___ ___ 山
7 忄 ___ ___ 忄 *or* 心 ___ ___ ___ 心
8 言 ___ ___ ___ ___ ___ ___ 言

How did you get on? Check your answers in the Key to the exercises at the back of the book.

We're going to help you with the next ones to make sure you understand the stroke order correctly.

車 follows the basic rules, first horizontal then vertical and from top to bottom but there is an additional point to remember. When the vertical goes *through* the horizontal(s), it (the vertical) is done *last*:

一 厂 帀 百 盲 亘 車

羊 also follows this rule:

丶 丷 丄 䒑 䒑 羊

毛 and 舌 both start with the same stroke ノ which was the second stroke in 羊 above:

毛 一 三 三 毛

舌 一 三 千 千 舌 舌

力 is written 丁 力.

女 is an interesting character. It originally came from the picture of a woman in a traditional, respectful position with her arms crossed over her stomach:

委 → ㄥ 女 女

子 whose origins we looked at in Unit 1, is written as follows: 乛 了 子. When used as a radical on the left-hand side, the last stroke is not horizontal but rising. Nevertheless, it moves in the same direction as the horizontal.

扌 has both these strokes in it:

一 寸 扌

Have a go at the next six yourself. Each line represents one stroke. They're a little trickier than the ones you did before so we'll give you a little help now and again:

╱ is in fact the radical 刀 *dāo* (knife) but is made much smaller and more stylised when it appears on the top of a character as it does here.

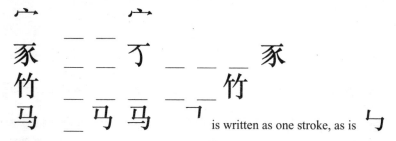

┐ is written as one stroke, as is 勹

ʌʌ only appears as 竹 when it actually stands for the plant bamboo but as the meaning or radical for other characters, it is written ʌʌ which is, fortunately, much simpler! The same is true for the grass radical. It is 草 when written on its own and means 'grass' but is written as 艹 (一 十 艹) when it is acting as a radical.

You may need some help with the last ones: 火 can either be written 丶丿丷火 (left to right rule), or 丶丶丿丷火 (top to bottom rule). 灬 is, of course, written 丶 灬 灬 灬.

辶 counts as *three* strokes: 丶 辶 辶 and is always written *last* no matter where it occurs in the character. This is probably because its last stroke finishes up right at the bottom of the character.

☑ Exercise 2

Let's do some more practice on the basic strokes you have learnt in this unit. In the table are five of these. Circle the stroke illustrated in the

column on the left in each of the characters which follow. We have done
one for you to show you what is required.

丿	小	材	少	尘	你
丶	心	言	家	米	兴
㇇	打	河	冰	牲	跑
丿	力	长	火	户	石
一	大	舌	草	鱼	马

Each individual Chinese character occupies exactly the same amount of
space, i.e. a square of the same proportions, whether it is imaginary or
real. Chinese children start writing characters on pages of squared paper
in order to maintain a better sense of proportion and balance. We have
provided you with a sample page to practise on. You might like to copy it
first before you write on it so that you use it again in the future. You can
make your own squared paper, with squares larger or smaller than the
ones we have given you.

There are other ways of improving your writing of characters:

- Write the characters LARGE and small to appreciate the proportions
  and balance within each character (use different sizes of squared paper
  for this).
- Write them fast. Copy or write twenty different characters as fast as
  you can for, say, three minutes, and see how many you can write. Do it
  again after you've done some practice (e.g. two weeks later) and see if
  you can write more characters within the same length of time. The
  purpose of this exercise is to give you confidence and help you maintain
  the flow of your writing.

☑ Exercise 3

Now that you have learned the basic rules about stroke order, how would
you write the following characters?

Example: 水   亅   才   水   水
1 月   ___ ___ ___   月
2 牛   ___ ___ ___   牛
3 户   ___ ___ ___   户
4 穴   ___ ___ ___ ___   穴
5 当   ___ ___ ___ ___ ___   当
6 米   ___ ___ ___ ___ ___   米

Not only does each Chinese character occupy the same amount of space, whether it is a very easy character e.g. 日 or a relatively complex one, e.g. 碗 *wǎn* (bowl), it must be in the right proportions. This does not mean that you have to do any measuring of any kind, it is basically what is pleasing to the eye. Simple points to remember are that both 'halves' must be roughly level at the top and bottom but there are notable exceptions to this. The radical 口 *kǒu* (mouth) (like a small enclosure 口) usually occurs on the left side of a character slightly lower than what is on the right-hand side, again for aesthetic purposes e.g. 吃 *chī* (to eat) would look very ugly if it were written 吃 or even 吃.

✔ Exercise 4

Look at the pairs of characters and circle the one in each pair which you think is better written.

A   a   B   b   C   c
大   大   好   好   月   月

D   d   E   e   F   f
火   火   弓   弓   水   水

Some characters do look similar. This may cause confusion and make it difficult for you to remember. However, it is important to spot the differences.

Can you see the difference(s) between the following pairs of characters? We have also provided you with the stroke order for each character.

人 (person) 丿 人   入 (to enter)   丿 入
广 (broad)   丶 亠 广   厂 (factory)   一 厂
彐 (tricky) フ 彐   习 (to practise)   フ 习 习

己 (self)	㇆ コ 己	已 (already)	㇆ コ 已
干 (to do)	一 二 干	于 (at, in)	一 二 于
贝 (shell)	丨 冂 贝 贝	见 (to see)	丨 冂 贝 见
东 (east)	一 𠂉 车 东 东	车 (vehicle)	一 𠂉 车 车
石 (stone)	一 ㄏ 不 石 石	后 (rear; behind)	一 厂 斤 斤 后 后
我 (I, me)	一 二 于 手 我 我 我	找 (to look for)	一 十 扌 扌 找 找 找

Another rule about stroke order which is worth remembering is that the dot ˋ in such characters as 我 and 找 always comes last. If it occurs inside an enclosure 口, however, it becomes the penultimate stroke, not the very last e.g. in 国 *guó* (country) the stroke order is:

国 also illustrates a refinement to the basic rule, first horizontal then vertical. As you have seen, the vertical stroke is done *before* the last horizontal one i.e. 干王 and not 三王. Remember that the vertical is done last when it *goes through* the last horizontal but not when it just touches it. So 三丰 but 干王.

Exercise 5

What is wrong with the following characters? (You have met them all in their correct form.)

A B C D E F G H

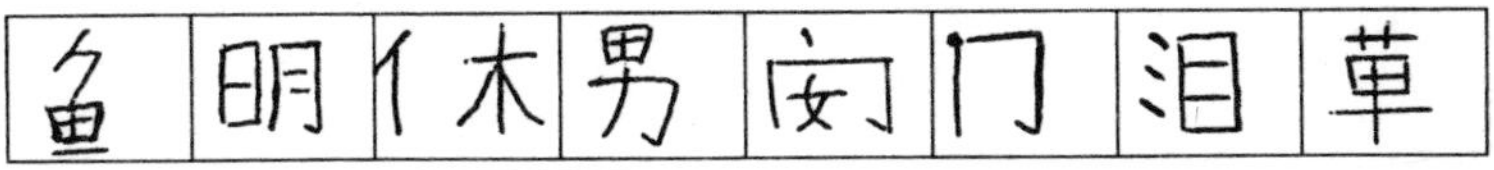

Now for some more radicals. In Unit 2, we introduced the concept of radicals. Do you remember what a radical is?

Exercise 6

What is a radical? Is it a:

a) stroke in a character b) character component c) simple character?

We have seen how most Chinese characters are made up of two components
– a radical and a phonetic. Radicals may be helpful in identifying the
general area of meaning of the character but this is not always apparent.
However, the radical will *always* help us find a particular character in a
dictionary and hence its actual meaning (see Unit 10). For that reason, we
need to learn as many of them as we can.

☑ Exercise 7

What do these radicals mean? Can you infer their meanings from the
translations given for each of the characters?

Meaning

1 目： 眼 eye　　　盯 to stare　　瞎 blind　　　眨 to blink _____
2 犭： 狗 dog　　　狼 wolf　　　猫 cat　　　　狐 fox _____
3 饣： 饱 full up　　饭 meal　　　饼 pancake　　馅 stuffing _____
4 刂： 刻 to carve　剁 to chop　　割 to cut　　　刺 to pierce _____
5 山： 峰 peak　　　岭 hill　　　崖 cliff　　　　岗 hill _____

☑ Exercise 8

Can you identify the radicals in the following characters? Write down the
radical of each character in the space provided and say what the character
might be to do with. Then check the Key to the exercises and see if you
got them right. You can find out what the characters actually mean in the
Chinese–English vocabulary at the back of the book.

Example:

Character　　*Radical*　　*Might have something to do with*
话　　　　　言(讠)　　　speech

1 枫 _____　　2 讽 _____　　3 峰 _____
4 海 _____　　5 晚 _____　　6 煮 _____
7 资 _____　　8 烧 _____　　9 笔 _____
10 刻 _____

☑ Exercise 9

Here are some more for you to remember (some have already appeared in
this unit):

Radical	Pinyin	Meaning	Radical	Pinyin	Meaning
刂 (刀)	*dāo*	knife	石	*shí*	stone, mineral
饣 (食)	*shí*	food	口	*kǒu*	mouth
目	*mù*	eye	贝	*bèi*	shell
氵 (水)	*shuǐ*	water	见	*jiàn*	to see
牛 (牜)	*niú*	cattle	页	*yè*	page
彳		step with left foot	米	*mǐ*	rice (uncooked)

Try working out the stroke order for each of them and then check it in the Key to the exercises. We have deliberately put 贝 *bèi*, 见 *jiàn* and 页 *yè* together to show you how similar they are in one sense and how different they are in meaning. It may help you to think of 贝 *bèi* as being written with 'straight' legs whereas 见 *jiàn* is written with one 'curly' one. 页 *yè* is just like 贝 *bèi* but it has ⌐ on top of it.

We have already noted that many radicals are to be found in the same position in any of the characters in which they occur. Look at the position of the various radicals in Exercises 7 and 8 and then do Exercise 10.

☑ **Exercise 10**

Where does the radical normally go?

1 马 (horse)   the left-hand side
2 艹 (grass/plant)   _____
3 犭 (animal)   _____
4 讠 (speech)   _____
5 灬 (fire)   _____
6 ⺮ (bamboo)   _____
7 氵 (water)   _____
8 刂 (knife)   _____
9 亻 (person)   _____
10 口 (mouth)   _____

☑ **Exercise 11**

Can you write the character according to the following description? Please
guess or give the meaning of the character if you can.

Description	*Character*	*Meaning*
1 Water in an eye (left and right)	_____	_____
2 Two trees next to each other	_____	_____
3 Bamboo with fur/hair underneath	_____	_____
4 A person in an enclosure	_____	_____
5 Fire under roof	_____	_____
6 Small (top) earth (bottom)	_____	_____
7 Sun (top) above light (光)	_____	_____

☑ **Exercise 12**

Group together all the characters that have the same radical. Number the
groups from 1–9 (there are nine groups altogether). What does the radical
in each group mean? (The answers will be in the Key to the exercises but
not necessarily in the order you have given them. When you have studied
Unit 10, you should be able to look up the characters you don't know in
a Chinese–English dictionary.)

泪 1	昨 __	吃 __	林 __	推 __	叮 __
诗 __	饭 __	汗 1	时 __	贵 __	材 __
杂 __	货 __	饺 __	喝 __	河 1	扣 __
别 __	刚 __	贡 __	词 __	晚 __	饿 __
打 __	吸 __	说 __	根 __	刷 __	订 __

1 <u>water</u>	2 _____	3 _____
4 _____	5 _____	6 _____
7 _____	8 _____	9 _____

's of combining single characters to form tw⟋
three- and four-character words. Here are son⟋

⟋peech = 电话 telephone

⟋ir = 天气 weather

⟋e radicals in their own right.

		Meaning
vehicle	火车	_____
worker	木工	_____
ticket	月票	_____
vision	电视	_____
vehicle	电车	_____
shadow	电影	_____
brain	电脑	_____

to listen = 好听 pleasant to listen to

to eat = 难吃 awful (food)

⟋e can also function as verbs so 好 *hǎo* mean⟋
⟋'good'. Some people call such adjectives stativ⟋
⟋n in this way.

	Meaning
好吃	_____
难听	_____
好看	_____
难看	_____

☑ Exercise 13

How many strokes are there in these characters? They may be new to you. Do not worry about their meanings. See if you can identify the number of strokes in each character. Check the Key to the exercises at the back of the book where the strokes of these characters are illustrated (cf. how to use a Chinese dictionary in Unit 10).

方 山 九 足 去 气 尺 风

学写字 Learning to write

A Chinese child started to learn writing on his first day with his teacher. The teacher began by showing him how to write 一, the character for 'one'. The child said to himself: 'That was easy.' Then the teacher taught him to write 二, the character for two. Seeing how easy it was to do two, the child became restless. Then he was shown how to write 三, the character for three. Before he was asked to write it, he shouted in protest: 'I know how to write now!' The teacher said to him: 'You are a quick learner. So much for the lesson. Your homework for today is to write the character for ten thousand.'

There are different w...
character words or eve...
examples.

Noun + noun

电 electric(ity) + 话...
天 day, sky + 气...

NB: Both 天 and 气...

In Units 1–3, we sa...
are combined to fo...
characters are co...
characters in the fi...

Let us look first at...
with those in Colu...
English next to the...
out the meanings f...

Column A	Co...
人 person	口...
入 to enter	口...
天 heaven/sky	子...
王 king	子...
工 work	人...
大 big	人...
小 small	人...

These words are reas...

Exercise 1

What do you think th...
the back of the book...

Column A
1 小 small
2 放 put down
3 瞎 blind
4 下 go downward

Exercise 2

1 火 fire
2 木 wood
3 月 moon
4 电 electric(ity)
5 电
6 电
7 电

Adjective* + ve...

好 good
难 hard, difficult...

* Adjectives in C...
'to be good' as we...
verbs when they f...

Exercise 3

1 好　吃
2 难　听
3 好　看 to loo...
4 难　看

Adjective + noun

小 small + 学 study = 小学 primary school
公 public + 园 enclosure = 公园 park

☑ Exercise 4

Meaning
1 大 big 学 to learn 大学 _____
2 花 flower 园 enclosure 花园 _____
3 好 good 心 heart; mind 好心 _____

☑ Exercise 5

公 public + 平 level = 公平

Does it mean:
a) to be fair; justice
b) scales
c) flat road?

明 bright + 天 day, sky = 明天

Does it mean:
a) yesterday
b) today
c) tomorrow?

Verb + verb

听 to listen + 说 to speak = 听说 to hear someone say
听 to listen + 懂 to understand = 听懂 to understand (through listening)
看 to look at + 懂 to understand = 看懂 to understand (through reading)
看 to look at + 见 to see = 看见 to have perceived by seeing (to have seen)
听 to listen + 见 to see = 听见 to have perceived by hearing (to have heard)

Verb + object

开 to start + 车 vehicle = 开车 to drive (a vehicle)
念 to read aloud + 书 book = 念书 to study

☑ Exercise 6

What do you think the following verb-objects mean?

Meaning

1 吃 to eat   饭 cooked rice   吃饭 _____
2 教 to teach 书 book   教书 _____
3 录 to record 音 sound   录音 _____
4 走 to walk   路 road   走路 _____
5 说 to speak 话 speech   说话 _____

As you can see from the last exercise, Chinese uses an object where you would not normally find one in English. Thus the English 'to eat' becomes 吃饭 'to eat cooked rice' in Chinese. This is because classical Chinese was monosyllabic (one-syllabled) whereas modern Chinese has become increasingly disyllabic (two syllabled) so the verb-object construction can be seen as conforming to this trend. Using the 'fill-in' object also produces a more balanced sentence from the Chinese point of view. Of course, if the verb has a 'proper' object then the 'fill-in' object is discarded e.g. 他 (he) 吃鱼 'He eats fish' (where 'fish' is the object).

Duplicates for plurals

Do you remember what 人 means? Yes, it is 'person'. What then do you think 人人 means? It means 'everybody'. Logical, isn't it? When some words are repeated, the meaning is 'every' plus the noun in question. But not all nouns work in this way. Let us look at some more examples:

天: day   天天 every day
月: month   月月 every month
年: year   年年 every year
代: generation 代代 every generation

How to write the numbers

Let's try writing the numbers 1 to 10.

一	二*	三	四	五	六	七	八	九	十*
yī	*èr*	*sān*	*sì*	*wǔ*	*liù*	*qī*	*bā*	*jiǔ*	*shí*

* 二 and 十 are both radicals in their own right.

Stroke order: points to remember

a) Remember that horizontal lines are done from left to right.
b) From top to bottom. (三) ⁻ ⁼ 三
c) Finish what is inside the box before closing the box. (四) 丨冂冂四四
d) Horizontal before vertical. (五) ⁻ 丁 五 五
e) Left falling before right falling. (六) 丶 亠 六 六
f) 乙 counts as one stroke. (九) 丿 九 Some people write it as ㇠九.
The important thing is for *you* to always write it the same way.

Pronunciation and the Chinese script

This book is about the Chinese script so we have decided not to spend a lot of time (and space) explaining the pronunciation to you. Please refer to *Teach Yourself Chinese* and *Teach Yourself Beginner's Chinese* if you want to learn to speak Chinese. In any case, spoken Chinese comes in many different dialects, the difference between many of them being greater than the difference between, say, English and German or Portuguese and Italian. The Chinese script, however, remains the same for all of these dialects, the only difference being that since the People's Republic of China came into being in 1949, the government has simplified a number of common characters (well over 2,000) in an attempt to raise literacy levels in China. Until then, characters had remained virtually unchanged for about 2,000 years. Officially, Taiwan and Hong Kong do not use these simplified characters but some are used unofficially, for example when people write to one another and so on. Singapore has adopted the simplified system.

The dialect whose pronunciation system is adopted in this book, as well as in *Teach Yourself Chinese* and *Teach Yourself Beginner's Chinese* is called *pǔtōnghuà* 普通话 'common speech'. It is sometimes referred to in the West as Modern Standard Chinese or Mandarin. More than 70% of Chinese people in the People's Republic of China speak some form of this dialect. It is also the official Chinese language or dialect in Taiwan and Singapore where it is known as *guóyǔ* 国语 'national language' and *huáyǔ* 华语 'Chinese (old word) language' respectively.

A simple guide to pronunciation can be found at the back of the book.

Once you have learned the numbers 1 to 10, you will be able to read and write 11 to 99.

11 is	$10 + 1 =$ 十一	41 is	$4 \times 10 + 1 =$ 四十一
12 is	$10 + 2 =$ 十二	52 is	$5 \times 10 + 2 =$ 五十二
19 is	$10 + 9 =$ 十九	87 is	$8 \times 10 + 7 =$ 八十七
20 is	$2 \times 10 =$ 二十	99 is	$9 \times 10 + 9 =$ 九十九
30 is	$3 \times 10 =$ 三十		

☑ Exercise 7

What numbers do the following characters represent?

(a) 四   (e) 九   (i) 三十五
(b) 八   (f) 六   (j) 九十四
(c) 五   (g) 十   (k) 七十六
(d) 七   (h) 十八   (l) 五十九

☑ Exercise 8

Try writing out the following numbers in Chinese characters. Don't forget your stroke order rules (cf. pp. 13). You can use the squared paper provided on pp. 24. This will help you to keep the characters the same size and with the correct spacing.

(a) 8   (c) 7   (e) 6   (g) 4   (i) 32   (k) 65
(b) 10   (d) 5   (f) 9   (h) 21   (j) 87   (l) 94

Although Arabic numbers are widely used in documents and newspaper articles, this traditional form of written numbers is still commonly used. In English, people use A, B, C, D for listing points. In Chinese, people tend to use 一二三四 for the same purpose. 第 in front of a number makes it into an ordinal (or ranking) number like first, ninth, etc. 第 has bamboo on top and the phonetic *di* underneath. It is written:

The equivalents to English first, second and third are 第(dì)一, 第二, and 第三 and not 第1, 第2, and 第3.

How to write the years

It is very easy to write the years in Chinese. Each figure is treated as a single number. Thus 1998 is said and written as 一九九八 with the character for year 年 *nián* written after it. 年 is written: ノ 广 乍 仁 乍 年.

Exercise 9

What are the following years?

(a) 一九一九 ____   (f) 一九一四 ____

(b) 一九九一 ____   (g) 一四九二 ____

(c) 一九四五 ____   (h) 一八四八 ____

(d) 一〇*六六 ____   (i) 二〇一五 ____

(e) 一七八九 ____

* Zero is the exception to the rule that Chinese characters are commonly used for writing numbers. The character for zero 零 is quite complicated so 〇 has been widely adopted instead.

Exercise 10

Write out the following years in Chinese characters (you don't need to write 年 after each one):

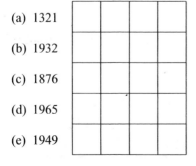

(a) 1321   (f) 1486

(b) 1932   (g) 1937

(c) 1876   (h) 1842

(d) 1965   (i) 2037

(e) 1949

How to write the date

We have already come across the characters for sun and moon. They are
日 and 月. Understandably 日 and 月 also represent day and month
respectively. Now, can you understand what the following dates are?

(a) 一月三日   (b) 十月八日   (c) 十二月二十五日

They are 3 January, 8 October and 25 December. This is really quite easy
and completely logical but have you noticed that in Chinese, the month
comes first? This is because the Chinese have a vertical rather than a
linear concept of time and move from the general to the particular so the
order is year, month, day, time of day (am/pm), hour, minute which is the
exact reverse of the English word order.

It should be noted that although in most informal writing, people use
Arabic numbers for dates, in most formal writing, dates are still written
in characters as in the examples we have just seen.

Learning tip: making your own flash cards

You can make your own flash cards as you work your way through the
book. It would be a good idea to go back to Unit 1 and make them for
Units 1–3 as well, as they contain a lot of useful, basic vocabulary.

A flash card normally consists of the character or characters on one side
and the English and/or romanisation on the other. A good size for your
flash card is 3cm.

Character	Reverse side	
火	fire	(*huǒ*)
明	bright	(*míng*) or bright (sun + moon)

You could also put on the reverse side how the character is made up (see
above), this might help you to remember it more easily.

Having made your flash cards (and of course you keep adding to them as
you learn new characters), you work through them looking at the character

side first and seeing how many of them you recognise. Check your answers with the English on the back. Put the ones you get right on one side and then work your way through the ones you got wrong, repeating the process until you recognise them all.

Having gone through your flash cards 'recognising' the characters, do it the other way round. Look at the side with the English and the explanation as to how the character is made up and try writing out the character itself. This is, of course, much harder! Check your answer with the character on the other side. Adopt the same system as before, putting aside the ones you get right and repeating the ones you get wrong.

You will probably need to do this many, many times before you have mastered them and as you add new flash cards to the old ones, there is always more to be done.

Find a handy sized box to keep your cards in, so that you can work on them on the bus, train or underground or in any spare moments you might have. You will be interested to know that even very young Chinese children learn their basic characters in this way. They used to have pictures on the front and characters on the back. The *pinyin* might be on the front or the back. The latest ones for learning characters also have English on the back!

A1	B1	C1	D1
难	钱	星期	电话
A2 *nán* difficult	**B2** *qián* money	**C2** *xīngqī* week	**D2** *diànhuà* telephone

A1	B1	C1	D1
学习	汉字	生词	卡片
A2	**B2**	**C2**	**D2**
xuéxí	*hànzì*	*shēngcí*	*kǎpiàn*
study	Chinese character	new words	card

Are you ready to read and write some more dates? Try the following exercises.

☑ **Exercise 11**

Can you recognise the following dates?

(a) 二月一日　(d) 四月十日　(g) 十一月二十六日

(b) 三月七日　(e) 六月二十日　(h) 十月十五日

(c) 五月九日　(f) 八月三十日　(i) 十二月三十一日

☑ **Exercise 12**

Match the English with their Chinese equivalents. We have done one for you.

(a) December　(e) 十一月　(f) May　　( ) 六月

(b) April　　( ) 八月　(g) July　　(e) 九月

(c) September ( ) 七月　(h) October ( ) 十二月

(d) June　　(^) 十月　(i) August　( ) 四月

(e) November ( ) 五月

☑ Exercise 13

Can you write out the following dates in Chinese characters?

a) New Year's Day
   (1st January)

b) St George's Day
   (23rd March)

c) American Independence Day
   (4th July)

d) Christmas Day
   (25th December)

e) Summer Solstice
   (21st June)

☑ Exercise 14

The cartoon depicts a man giving his wife flowers for International Women's Day. What is the date of this special day?

How to write the days of the week

All you need to know to write the characters for the days of the week are the two characters 星 *xīng* (star) and 期 *qī* (period) which, when combined together, form the word for week; plus the numbers 1 to 6 and the characters for sun 日 (*rì*) or day 天 (*tiān*). 星 *xīng* is made up of the radical 日 *rì* (sun) and 生 *shēng* (to give birth).

We have given you the correct stroke order in the boxes:

期 *qī* is made up of the phonetic element 其 *qí* (its) and the radical 月 *yuè* (moon).

Practise writing the days of the week on your own. You have already met 日 *rì* (sun) and 天 *tiān* (day).

✅ Exercise 15

Match the Chinese with their English equivalents.

1 星期一 ( ) Thursday   5 星期五 ( ) Wednesday
2 星期二 ( ) Saturday   6 星期六 ( ) Sunday
3 星期三 ( ) Friday   7 星期日 ( ) Tuesday
4 星期四 ( ) Monday

✅ Exercise 16

Write the number in the space which gives you the correct day in answer to the following questions:

Example:
   Which day comes two days before Thursday?   星期二

a) Which day comes after Wednesday?   星期____

b) Which day comes before Tuesday?   星期____

c) Which day do Jewish people go to the synagogue?   星期____

MINI-TEST

You may find some of the exercises in the mini-test quite challenging. You may like to return to them after you have finished the book. Hopefully you will be amazed by the progress you have made.

Exercise 1

We have learned that in many characters there is one component which indicates the pronunciation. That component is called the sound component. Now that you have learned a number of meaning radicals, see if you can match the characters with their respective meaning in the following exercise. These characters sound very similar because they all share the same sound component 青 *qīng*. Put the appropriate number in the brackets. We have done one for you.

1 情 *qíng* ( ) to ask, to request   5 蜻 *qīng* ( ) cyanogen
2 清 *qīng* ( ) dragonfly   6 晴 *qíng* ( ) mackerel
3 鲭 *qīng* ( ) bright/sunny day   7 氰 *qíng* (2) clear
4 请 *qīng* ( ) feeling

Exercise 2

Identify the Chinese phrases and write the correct number in the bracket in front of their English translation. We have done one for you.

1 人民大会堂   ( ) People's Square
2 人民币   ( ) People's Park
3 人民日报   ( ) Great Hall of the People
4 人民公园   ( ) People's Daily
5 人民广场   (2) Chinese currency

Exercise 3

What do you think the following words mean? Do they mean a), b) or c)? Circle what you think is the correct answer. (The dictionary definition of each individual character is provided.)

生日   a) sunrise   b) birthday   c) early morning
        生 to be born; raw   日 sun; day
早安   a) dawn   b) settlement   c) good morning
        早 early   安 peace; put in place
日历   a) diary   b) calendar   c) rainbow
        日 sun; day   历 history

☑ Exercise 4

Try and fill in the missing characters in the captions above the picture.
We have tried to help you by giving you the basic meaning of each of the
characters you will need to use. 午 occurs more than once.

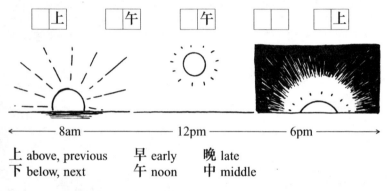

<- 8am ————————— 12pm ————————— 6pm ->

上 above, previous   早 early   晚 late
下 below, next   午 noon   中 middle

☑ Exercise 5

Guess what the caption below the cartoon means. You have already met the
word 公平 earlier in this chapter. Can you find it again? (不 *bù* means
'not' and is put in front of all verbs except 有 *yǒu* (to have) to negate them.)

不公平
Which side of the shop window is menswear?

✅ **Exercise 6**

Some characters occur as part of many different words. 中 (middle) and
火 (fire) are good examples of this. What do you think the following words
mean? For each word, choose what you think is the correct translation
from the list on the right and write it in the blank space provided

a)
中学 _____
中国 _____
中心 _____
中午 _____

noon
centre
Chinese language
Chinese newspaper
China
secondary school

b)
火腿 (leg) _____
火山 _____
火车 _____
火箭 (arrow) _____
火花 _____

rocket
torch
spark
volcano
fireworks
train
ham

Cultural tip:
风 wind + 水 water = 风水 wind and water?

风水 *fēngshuǐ* actually means geomancy. Early Chinese belief (and one
which is still held by many Chinese throughout the world) holds that the
spirits of land, water and wind played an active part in human affairs.
Thus, the location and the direction in which a house or tomb faces,
and even the position of the windows and furniture within the home are
of the utmost importance. They determine the fortunes of the family
which occupies the house or the relatives of the dead person. Tombs,
for example, should face south with protecting hills behind them and a
river or stream nearby so that good luck can flow to the family of the
deceased.

The idea behind this is that people are part of the natural order; therefore,
where they build their dwellings or graves must harmonise with the forces
that exist in nature. Even some businesses (including non-Chinese ones)
take 风水 into account when deciding on the height and exact location

of their premises in an attempt to cut off the flow of good luck to their competitors. This is achieved by such measures as blocking out the sunlight to their offices and/or casting a shadow on them.

I told you the *fengshui* here was no good.

我说过这儿的风水不好。

✅ Exercise 7

What is the radical for the following words? Please write it in the space provided. (2) means you should try and write the two versions of the radical.

a) mouth ____ b) rain ____ c) fire (2) ____ ____
d) page ____ e) wind ____ f) knife (2) ____ ____
g) rice ____ h) child ____ i) metal (2) ____ ____
j) eye ____ k) horse ____ l) speech (2) ____ ____
m) big ____ n) field ____ o) heart (2) ____ ____
p) woman ____ q) mountain ____ r) step with
s) door ____ t) to walk ____   left foot ____

Finally, here are fourteen more radicals for you to learn:

Radical	Pinyin	Meaning	Radical	Pinyin	Meaning
八 or ⸂	bā	eight	纟	sī	silk
天	tiān	day, heaven	衣 (衤)	yī	clothing
王	wáng	king	冰 (冫)	bīng	ice
门	mén	door	禾	hé	grain, plant
风	fēng	wind	穴	xué	cave, hole
虫	chóng	insect	气	qì	air
广	guǎng	covering, roof	犭	quǎn	(wild) animal, dog

The stroke order for these is fairly straightforward:

八 丿 八 or ⸢ ⸣ ⸄

天 一 二 于 天

王 一 二 干 王

门 丶 丬 门

风 丿 几 风 风

虫 丨 ⼝ 口 中 虫 虫

广 丶 ⼀ 广

纟 ⼥ ⼥ 纟

衣 丶 ⼀ 方 衣 衣 衣

永 　ﾟ　ﾌﾞ　永　永　永

冫　　ﾟ　冫

冰　　ﾟ　冫　冫]　冴　冰　冰

禾　　一　二　千　禾　禾

穴　　ﾟ　宀　宀　宀　穴

气　　ﾉ　ﾆ　气　气

犭　　ﾉ　犭　犭

Note the difference between 禾 grain and 天 day. In 禾 the first stroke is sloping ⌐ but it is horizontal 一 in 天.

5 | UNIT 5
| *Signs (1)*

From this unit on,
we are going to take you
through your business trip
to China. You are attending
a conference in Beijing,
and will do some
sightseeing and shopping.

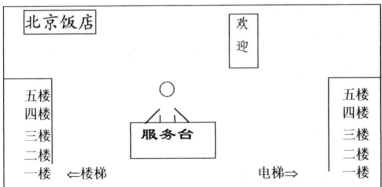

New words (the radical for each character is shown in brackets after it.)

北京	*Běijīng*	Beijing
	北	north	(丨 or 匕)
	京	capital	(亠)
饭店	*fàndiàn*	hotel; restaurant
	饭	rice, meal	(饣)
	店	shop	(广)
楼梯	*lóutī*	stairs
	楼	building	(木)
	梯	stairs	(木)

服务台	*fúwùtái*	reception	
服务		to serve; service	(月 力)
台		platform; station	(口)
服务员	*fúwùyuán*	attendant	
员		person	(口)
欢迎	*huānyíng*	to welcome	
欢		joyfully	(又)
迎		to greet	(辶)

☑ Exercise 1

Identify the new radicals (i.e. ones you *haven't* met in Units 1–4) in the new words in the list. Write them in the blanks that follow.

a) ___ ___

Radical Meaning

b) i)   What is the radical of 饭?   ___ ___
    ii) What is the radical of 楼?   ___ ___
    iii) What other two radicals (acting as the
         phonetic) occur on the right-hand side
         of 楼?   ___ ___
    iv) What is the component below ⊓ in 员?   ___ ___
    v)   Give the stroke order for 迎.   _____

c) Give the stroke order for 梯 (rather tricky). You had 弟 in Unit 4.
   木 ___ ___ ___ ___ ___ ___ ___ (梯)
   弟 *dì* means younger brother and is normally reduplicated i.e. 弟弟
   as are 爸爸* *bàba* (dad), 妈妈 *māma* (mum), 姐姐 *jiějie* (elder
   sister) and 哥哥 *gēge* (elder brother), 妹妹 *mèimei* (younger sister).

d) What is the radical for 妈妈? _____ For 姐姐? _____ For 哥哥?
   _____ For 妹妹? _____
   *父 *fù* is another new radical, meaning 'father' or elderly male person.

☑ Exercise 2

What do you think the following Chinese words mean?

电梯 (bottom right corner in the picture) _____
店员 (cf. 服务员) _____
服务楼   _____
电台 (cf. 服务台) _____

Cultural tip

The first floor in China is the ground floor in Britain, and the second floor in China is the first floor in Britain, and so on. America has the same system as China.

Exercise 3

Having settled down in your hotel room, you decide to have some lunch. There are two restaurants in the hotel. Follow the sign 餐厅 (canteen or restaurant) and you see a 服务员 giving you directions. You have a choice of two restaurants, Cantonese (*Guǎngdōng*) or Sichuan. Which is which?

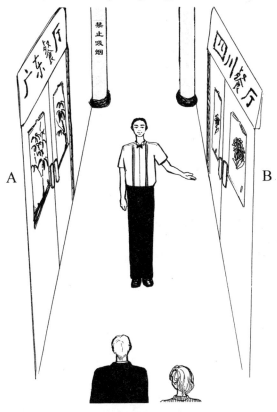

A: _____   B: _____

风味   flavour, style of cooking
  风 *fēng* wind   (风)
  味 *wèi*   taste, flavour   (口)

By the way there is a sign on the wall (**禁止吸烟**) asking you not to do
something. Is it asking you:

 (i) not to take photographs   (iii) not to dump litter
(ii) not to smoke   (iv) not to enter

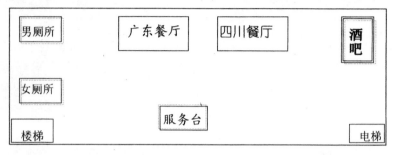

Now look at the hotel floor map. Can you find where the toilets are? Do
you remember 男 *nán* and 女 *nǚ* introduced in Unit 2? Yes, they are
'man' and 'woman'. The Chinese for 'toilet' is 厕所 *cèsuǒ*.

There is one more new word on the map. It is in the top right-hand
corner. You will come across it again soon. But look at the radical of the
first character and you may have an idea what it is.

At the conference

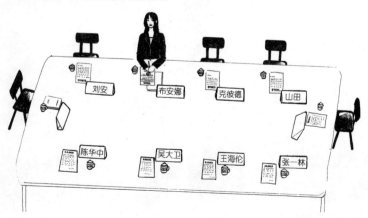

Common surnames include:

张　王　李　赵　刘　陈　林　吴　郭　郑
Zhāng　Wáng　Lǐ　Zhào　Liú　Chén　Lín　Wú　Guō　Zhèng

Note: they do not all appear in the illustration.

Cultural tip

These ten surnames are among the most common in China. While
Zhao, Liu, Wu are purely for people's names and place names, Zhang,
Wang, Li, Lin, Guo, Chen and Zheng have other meanings. As you
already know, 林 *lín* is 'forest' and 王 *wáng* is 'king'. 张 *zhāng*
means 'to stretch', and 李 *lǐ* is 'plum'.

中国	*Zhōngguó*	China	美国	*Měiguó*	United States
法国	*Fǎguó*	France	德国	*Déguó*	Germany
英国	*Yīngguó*	Britain	日本	*Rìběn*	Japan
台湾	*Táiwān*	Taiwan	香港	*Xiānggǎng*	Hong Kong
意大利	*Yìdàlì*	Italy	加拿大	*Jiānádà*	Canada

生词	***Shēngcí***	**New words**
中	centre, middle	中国: the Middle Kingdom
法	law, rule	*Fǎ* sounds similar to the first syllable of France
英	hero	*Yīng* sounds similar to the first syllable of England

美	beautiful	*Měi* sounds similar to the second syllable of America
		(the second syllable (i.e. *me*) of America is stressed, hence more prominent)
德	virtue	*Dé* sounds similar to the first syllable of Deutschland
香	fragrant	
港	harbour	

✔ Exercise 4

Match the participants with their nationalities.

王海伦 英国	山田 日本	李明芳 法国	张一林 中国	吴大卫 美国	刘安 香港

1 Who is from Japan? _____
2 Where is 吴大卫 from? _____
3 Is Ms Wang/King from China? _____
4 Which country does Ms Li represent? _____
5 Is there anybody from Germany? _____
6 What is the surname of the Hong Kong participant? _____

Cultural tip: translation of English names

English names, or any foreign names for that matter, are translated into Chinese mainly according to what they sound like to the Chinese ear. Chinese characters which sound similar are used to represent the sound. The table that follows gives some examples of this.

Another way of creating a Chinese name is to choose a character for one's surname and one or two characters for one's given name. (In Chinese the surname should come first, followed by one's given name and finally one's title when used.) The characters in one's Chinese name should ideally be close, both in terms of sound or meaning to the non-Chinese name. The surname, of course, should come first, and the first name should be second to make it resemble a Chinese name.

Some common English names and their Chinese translations

Given names	Pinyin	Characters	Given names	Pinyin	Characters
John	*Yuēhàn*	约翰	Clare	*Kèlái'ěr*	克莱尔
David	*Dàwèi*	大卫	Karen	*Kǎilún*	凯伦
Colin	*Kǎolín*	考林	Helen	*Hǎilún*	海伦
Peter	*Bǐdé*	彼德	Anna	*Ānnà*	安娜
Robert	*Luóbótè*	罗伯特	Jane	*Jiǎn*	简
Mark	*Mǎkè*	马克	Lisa	*Lìshā*	丽莎
Surnames					
Smith	*Shǐmìsī*	史密斯	Brown	*Bùlǎng*	布朗
Clinton	*Kèlíndùn*	克林顿	Green	*Gélín*	格林
Blair	*Bùlái'ěr*	布莱尔	Black	*Bùláikè*	布莱克

✔ Exercise 5

Your Chinese friends have told you what their names mean. Can you write down their names in characters?

A   'My surname is Liu. My given name is Guo'an. "Guo" means country
    and "an" means peace.' ___ ___
B   'Mum and Dad gave me the name of "big bright". They obviously
    hoped that I would be a star.' ___ ___
C   'My given name is Yinglin. "Ying" means hero while "lin" means
    forest.' ___ ___
D   'Because I was born in Beijing, I am called Jingsheng, literally
    meaning capital-born.' ___ ___

How to write the time

In Unit 4, we learned the Chinese characters for dates. Now let's look at
time. Try the next exercise first and work out what characters mean *hour*
(as on the clock), *minute*, *a quarter* (of an hour) and *half* (of an hour).
Circle one example of each (character) in the times given in the Chinese
below.

两*点半   三点一刻   三点五十五   五点四十五
两点三十分   三点十五分   差五分四点   五点三刻

* Note that 两 *liǎng* (two) is used where there are two of a kind, instead
of 二 *èr*.

The five new words used for expressing time are:

点 *diǎn* o'clock   分 *fēn* minute   刻 *kè* a quarter   半 *bàn* half   差 *chà*
lack; missing

Did you get them right? Let's take a closer look at these characters and
see if we can find a way of remembering them.

点 has the fire radical underneath. It also means to light a fire. When it
got dark, people would light a candle, hence it was to do with time. The
classical or complicated character for 点 is 點, which has 'dark' or
'black' on the left side. 分 means 'to divide', as expressed by a 刀 (knife)
which is the bottom radical of 分. The character then means division, and

was later used to represent a division of time. It is also used to represent the smallest unit of Chinese money. The right-hand side of 刻 is also a knife. It is called a vertical knife or a standing knife. 刻 means to carve or engrave, and as a noun it refers to a short period of time. 半, meaning half, is straightforward: a line cutting through the middle breaking it into two equal parts. 差 is made up of the radical for sheep 羊 *yáng* (slanted here) and the phonetic element 工 *gōng*. No help here for pronunciation, unfortunately.

Although Arabic numerals are widely used in China when expressing numbers, traditional characters like 八、九、十, are still used everywhere, especially in a formal context, such as the dates in a document as well as the times on a sign indicating the opening hours of a shop.

☑ Exercise 6

What are the opening hours of the following places?

| 中国银行 | 九点 ---- 十七点 | _____ |

| 森林餐厅 | 早七点 ---- 晚十一点 | _____ |

| 邮电局 | 八点半 ---- 十九点 | _____ |

| 办公室 | 上午八点 --- 十二点
下午两点 --- 六点 | _____ |

☑ Exercise 7

Now for some quick revision. What are the radicals of these characters? (Try not to refer to the explanations given earlier.)

a) 分 _____
b) 刻 _____
c) 半 _____
d) 钟 _____   (钟 *zhōng* means 'clock')
e) 差 _____

☑ Exercise 8

Write down in characters the time on each of the clocks:

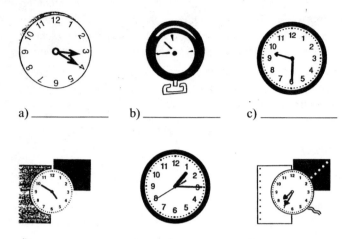

a) _____   b) _____   c) _____

d) _____   e) _____   f) _____

Now back to the conference. Saturday's and Sunday's itinerary for the
conference participants is shown in the following table.

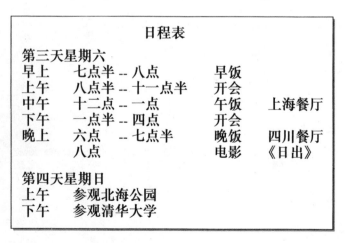

日程表

第三天星期六
早上   七点半 -- 八点   早饭
上午   八点半 -- 十一点半   开会
中午   十二点 -- 一点   午饭   上海餐厅
下午   一点半 -- 四点   开会
晚上   六点 -- 七点半   晚饭   四川餐厅
         八点   电影   《日出》

第四天星期日
上午   参观北海公园
下午   参观清华大学

生词	*Shēngcí*	New words
日程表	*rìchéngbiǎo*	itinerary
程		journey
表		form; table; watch
第	*dì*	ordinal number prefix (see Unit 4, page 30)
早上	*zǎoshang*	early morning
上午	*shàngwǔ*	morning
中午	*zhōngwǔ*	noon
下午	*xiàwǔ*	afternoon
晚上	*wǎnshang*	evening
上海	*Shànghǎi*	Shanghai
开会	*kāi huì*	hold a meeting
开		to open, to start
会		meeting
参观	*cānguān*	to visit
日出	*rìchū*	sunrise
出		to go/come out
北海	*běihǎi*	north sea
北		north (cf. 北京 at the beginning of this unit)
海		sea
公园	*gōngyuán*	park (cf. Unit 4, page 27)

☑ Exercise 9

What is the radical for:

程 ___ 表 ___ 第 ___ 早 ___ 上 ___ 中 ___ 午 ___
下 ___ 晚 ___ 开 ___ 会 ___ 参 ___ 观 ___ 海 ___
公 ___ 园 ___

☑ Exercise 10

Answer the following questions based on the itinerary we have just seen, first in English, then in characters where possible.

Characters

1 Where will you have lunch on Saturday? _____ _____
2 What will you do in the evening
   at 8 p.m.? _____ _____
3 When is lunch? _____ _____
4 When will the afternoon session start? _____ _____
5 Are you having a meeting on Saturday? _____ _____
6 What are you doing on Sunday morning? _____ _____
7 What kind of institution are you visiting
   on Sunday afternoon? _____ _____

☑ Exercise 11

It's 10pm after the film show. You might feel like going to the 酒吧 (bar) for a drink before going to bed.

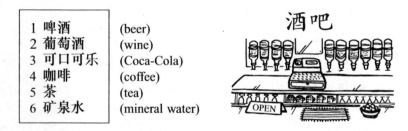

1 啤酒   (beer)
2 葡萄酒   (wine)
3 可口可乐   (Coca-Cola)
4 咖啡   (coffee)
5 茶   (tea)
6 矿泉水   (mineral water)

Look at the menu and identify the radicals in the characters. Do you think that the radicals make sense?

☑ Exercise 12

The English and Chinese on the following two signs have got confused. Can you put them right? What should the order of the English words be in a)?

a)

酒 吧 | 饮 料 | 餐 食
BEVERAGE | FOOD | BAR

_____   _____   _____

Now write out the correct sequence for the Chinese characters in b).

b)

✓ Exercise 13

Here is the layout of a hotel lobby. Can you identify what the various signs mean?

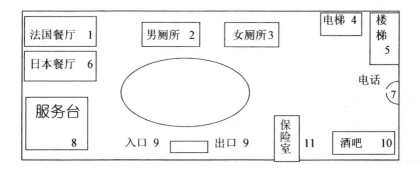

Give the English equivalent after each number as indicated in the picture:

1 _____ 2 _____ 3 _____
4 _____ 5 _____ 6 _____
7 _____ 8 _____ 9 _____
10 _____ 11 deposit boxes

Let's revise the radicals that have occurred for the first time in this unit and learn some more new ones.

Radical	Pinyin	Meaning	Radical	Pinyin	Meaning
宀		above	玉	yù	jade
又	yòu	again, also	寸	cùn	inch
父	fù	father	疒	bìng	illness
足	zú	foot	鸟	niǎo	bird (long-tailed)
走	zǒu	to go, walk	巾	jīn	towel, napkin
舟	zhōu	boat	立	lì	to stand
戈	gē	spear	礻		omen; to express
阝 on LHS		mound	酉	yǒu	spirit made from ripe millet; tenth of Twelve Earthly Branches*
阝 on RHS		town, region			
攵		to tap, rap			
方	fāng	square			

* If you would like to know more about the Earthly Branches and the Heavenly Stems and their connection with the Chinese zodiac, then refer to *Teach Yourself Chinese* pages 252–3.

6 UNIT 6
Signs (2)

Let's revise the radicals we have already learnt by recognising them in some of the characters we have met so far. Group together all the characters that have the same radical (there are ten groups in all). List all ten radicals below the box. Try and remember what each character means. You can check your answers in the Key to the exercises.

出 ___	下 ___	华 ___	梯 ___	北 ___	河 ___
湖 ___	园 ___	二 ___	上 ___	法 ___	东 ___
南 ___	楼 ___	香 ___	晚 _1_	弟 ___	分 ___
半 ___	三 ___	共 ___	海 ___	李 ___	十 ___
星 _1_	公 ___	汽 ___	国 ___	程 ___	中 ___

1 日 sun   2 _____   3 _____   4 _____   5 _____

6 _____   7 _____   8 _____   9 _____   10 _____

The conference is over. Time for some sightseeing. You decide to go to 香山公园, a beautiful park in the western suburbs of Beijing. You can either travel by 出租汽车 (taxi) or by 公共汽车 (bus). You may notice that both 'taxi' and 'bus' contain the word 汽车, which in fact means 'vehicle'.

出租汽车 (*chūzūqìchē*) taxi
  出租 for rent or hire
  – 出 out
  – 租 rent; to rent
  汽车 vehicle
  – 汽 steam, gas
  – 车 vehicle
公共汽车 (*gōnggòngqìchē*) bus
  公共 public
  – 公 public
  – 共 common; to share

Now would you be able to follow the sign and go to the right place to get on a bus or a taxi?

出租汽车站   公共汽车站   (开往香山)

Cultural tip

The word for bus is different depending on where you are. It is 公共汽车, or 汽车 for short, in the People's Republic of China. It is called 公车 (still a public vehicle as the characters suggest) in Taiwan. In Hong Kong, where Cantonese is spoken, a bus is called '*bāshi*', which is in fact how the locals pronounce 'bus'. The characters for '*bāshi*' are 巴士, which do not mean anything but represent the sound only. 巴士, however, is being increasingly used in China especially in Guangdong Province (Canton).

At the park entrance, you see a map of the park. You should be able to identify the places on the map. If you are not sure of any of them, just examine the radical(s) of the words carefully.

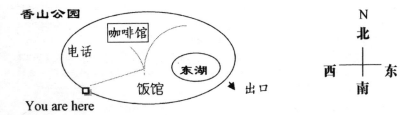

✓ Exercise 1

Check the signposts and answer the following questions (which your friend who has no knowledge of Chinese characters might ask you).

1 In which part of the park is the lake?
2 Which way will you turn if you want to have some hot drinks?
3 Where will you find a telephone kiosk?
4 If you decide to have a meal, which way should you turn?
5 Where is the exit?

Now let's learn the direction words. These words are not only often found in place names, but also in people's names.

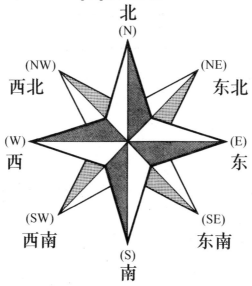

Cultural tip

Now you know the Chinese characters for China: 中国, the Middle Kingdom. The Chinese regarded China as at the centre of the world, hence the name.

When listing the cardinal points we say north, south, east, west, whereas the Chinese say 东南西北 (E, S, W, N) or 东西南北 (E, W, S, N) for the four directions. They also use the phrase 东西南北中 to refer to the whole country. There is a TV programme called 东西南北中 which introduces places of interest from all over China.

Do you remember the following words – 东南、东北、西南、西北?

Yes, they are SE, NE, SW and NW in English i.e. the reverse of the Chinese word order. Note the use of 、 between the items. This is known as a pause mark and is used in a list after each item where we would use a comma in English. A comma is reserved for longer pauses in Chinese.

The following Chinese cities/provinces all have direction words in them:

北京、西安、南京、河北、河南、山东、山西、广东、广西、湖南、湖北、海南、西藏

河	*hé*	river
广	*guǎng*	broad
湖	*hú*	lake
海	*hǎi*	sea
藏	*zàng*	the Zang (Tibetan) nationality

☑ Exercise 2

See how many places you can recognise on the map of China.

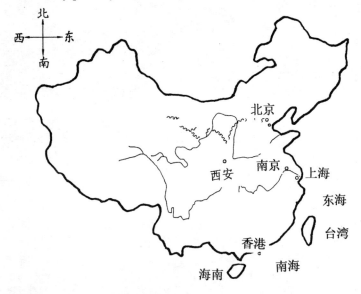

Cultural tip: Place names in China

河北、河南　The Yellow River divides the two provinces. One is
north of the river, hence 河北 and the other south of the river, hence
河南.

山东、山西　Taihang Mountain is between Shangdong and Shanxi
Provinces, hence the names 山东, east of the mountain(s) and 山西
west of the mountain(s).

湖南、湖北　Hubei and Hunan Provinces are north and south of
洞庭湖 Dongting Lake, one of the biggest lakes in China.

Exercise 3

Do you know where these places are?

1 中东   3 南美
2 地中海   4 北海 (near the UK)

Exercise 4

Match the road signs with their correct *pinyin* equivalents:

a)

b)

c)

1 Zhongshan Bei Lu   _____
2 Ren He Lu   _____
3 Ping Hai Lu   _____

Exercise 5

i) On the photo of
   Zhongshan Bei Lu,
   in which direction will
   you be going if you
   go left?
   _____

ii) If you go right?
   _____

iii) In which city was the
   photo on the right
   taken?

✔ Exercise 6

Match the requests in Column A with the characters in Column B. Where should someone go when:

A   B
a) s/he wants a drink   i) 电话
b) s/he wants to go to the toilet   ii) 饭馆
c) s/he wants to have a meal   iii) 酒吧
d) s/he wants to make a telephone call   iv) 厕所

✔ Exercise 7

Match up the English notice with its correct Chinese equivalent. We have done one for you.

a) Exit ( )   b) Toilets   ( )   c) No smoking   ( )
d) Taxi ( )   e) Duty-Free   (2)   f) Flower Shop ( )
g) British Education Exhibition ( )

1)

2)

3)

4)

5)

6)

7)

98英国教育展

⚡ Exercise 8

What should you do or not do when you see the following signs?
Sometimes you may only recognise one character in the sign but believe
it or not, you can still do the exercise!

(a) 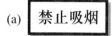   (b) 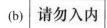   (c)

⚡ Exercise 9

Can you spot the mistakes in these phrases? Circle the incorrect character
and write its correct form in the blank(s) after the phrase. Look at the
cartoon below if you are not sure.

a) 请勿昭相 _____   c) 请勿吸咽 _____
b) 小心解电 _____   d) 请勿随地灶痰 _____

No spitting   No smoking   No photography   Danger : Electric Shock

Formation of new characters

In Unit 2, we looked at various ways of creating new characters: radical
plus radical, radical plus phonetic. Here are two much less common
methods but ones which are of great interest. In the first group, one
component is the radical and the other component serves a double function,
representing both the meaning and the sound:

女 + 取 (*qǔ*) to obtain → 娶 (*qǔ*) to marry (as of a man taking a woman
    into his family)

女 + 家 (*jiā*) family, home → 嫁 (*jià*) to marry (as of a woman being
    taken into her husband's family)

These two examples also show us the patriarchal nature of traditional Chinese society. Women married into their husbands' families and it was customary to live with one's in-laws. It was only men from very poor families who could not afford to pay a bride price who moved into their wives' homes. This was considered to be very shameful and in such cases the children of the marriage would take their mother's family name. In this context, it is interesting to note that the character for 'treacherous' or 'traitor' was 姦 (*jiān*), it also meant 'adultery'. It is now written 奸 but nevertheless the fact remains that the radical is 女. The character for slave 奴 (*nú*) also has a female radical.

In the second group, two separate characters (not always radicals) are put together to form new characters. The meaning of the new character is directly related to both of the original characters. Do you remember 不 *bù* (not) in 不公平?

不 + 正 *zhèng* (straight) = 歪 *wāi* (crooked)
不 + 好 *hǎo* (good)　　 = 孬 *nāo* (bad)
不 + 用 *yòng* (use)　　 = 甭 *béng* (don't)
不 + 口 *kǒu* (mouth)　 = 否 *fǒu* (deny; or not) (as in 是否 'whether
　　　　　　　　　　　　　　 or not')

The pronunciation of such characters is interesting. The pronunciation of 歪 *wāi* bears no resemblance to *bù* or *zhèng* but sounds suitably crooked. The other three have taken on some of their "parents'" characteristics!

☑ Exercise 10

Which radical is missing? (The following words mean upstairs, bank, bar and restaurant.)

a) 娄上　　　　　　　　c) 酉吧
b) 艮行　　　　　　　　d) 反店

☑ Exercise 11

Fill in the blanks with appropriate characters. (The following words mean train station, wine, mineral water and attendant.)

a) 火__站　　　　　　　c) 矿__水
b) 葡萄__　　　　　　　d) 服务__

☑ **Exercise 12**

Match the signs with their correct translation:

禁止停车   Peking University   北京大学   Bank of France

法国银行   Shanghai-bound train | 开往上海 | No parking

☑ **Exercise 13**

Complete the following passage by filling in the missing characters from the list provided. Each character may be used once only.

我 (*wǒ* I, me) 星期 _1_ 去 (*qù* to go) 北 _2_ 开 _3_ 。我们 (*wǒmen*, we) 下午两 _4_ 到 (*dào* to) 四点 _5_ 开会。晚 _6_ 八点三 _7_ 去看 (*kàn* to see) 电 _8_ 。明天 _9_ 期天我们去参 _10_ 北海公 _11_ 。

京 刻 影 观 园 上 点 会 星 半 六

☑ **Exercise 14**

Put the following Chinese sentences into the correct order as indicated in the passage in English:

I eat my breakfast at 6.30am. I *like* (喜欢 *xǐhuān*) drinking coffee. I don't eat rice for breakfast. I go *to work* (上班 *shàng bān*) at 7.15. I drive to work.

1 我早饭不吃米饭。
2 我开车上班。
3 我早上六点半吃早饭。
4 我喜欢喝咖啡。
5 我七点一刻去上班。

The correct order is:___ ___ ___ ___ ___ .

☑ Exercise 15

Translate the following passage into English:

我在 (*zài* at) 南京饭店住 (*zhù* to live) 四天。第一天服务员说
'欢迎你 (*nǐ* you singular) 来 (*lái* to come) 南京饭店住。'我
住三楼。第二天上午我去玄武 (*Xuánwǔ*) 湖公园参观，下午
去中山陵 (see picture)，晚上去看电影。第三、第四天在南京
大学开会。第三天中午在广东餐厅吃饭，第四天中午在
上海餐厅吃饭，都 (*dōu* both, all) 很 (*hěn* very) 好吃。第五天早上
七点吃早饭。七点三刻坐出租汽车去火车站，坐八点十分
的*火车回 (*huí* to return) 北京。

* 的: This character is required for grammatical purposes (cf. *Teach
Yourself Chinese* page 80). For this exercise you can ignore it, the meaning
of the phrase should still be clear.

中山陵 **Dr Sun Yatsen's Mausoleum**

7 UNIT 7
Signs (3)

Let's do some more work on signs. The ones in this exercise are much more difficult than those in Unit 6, but even if you only recognise one or two characters in each sign you should be able to match it with its English equivalent from the box below. We have done one for you. The English translations all come from real life!

✓ Exercise 1

a) 国际、香港到达   (　)
b) 吸烟室   (4)
c) 行李检查   (　)
d) 凭票入内   (　)
e) 欢迎使用太平洋信用卡   (　)
f) 办手续   (　)
g) 旅游投诉电话   (　)
h) 南京中国国际旅行社   (　)
i) 黄线范围内禁止停放车辆   (　)
j) 本区唯一书店   (　)

```
1  No More Book Shop Ahead
2  Baggage Inspection
3  No Parking Within the Yellow Lines
4  Smoking Lounges
5  Tourists' Complaint Hotline
6  International, Hong Kong Arrivals
7  Welcome to the Pacific Credit Card
8  No Entry Without Ticket
9  Check-In
10 Nanjing China International Travel Service
```

A selection of Chinese notices taken from real life follows. One of them is in full characters. Can you spot which?

i)

ii)

iv)

本區唯一書店

iii)

You now have a few days off before you fly home via Shanghai where you have some business to attend to. You decide you'd like to do some shopping. To save time, you take a taxi from the hotel. As you get into the front, you notice a sign on the front passenger's window: 前排客座只准坐女、兒*童. (* 兒 is the full form of the simplified character 儿 which means 'child/son' and is also a radical.) The driver points to the sign and indicates that you should sit in the back. Do you know why? (Men are not allowed in the front seats of taxis.)

You arrive at a large shopping mall. Look at the floor plan and then do the
following exercise. Your knowledge of radicals will come in handy here!

A 中国银行	D 山东饭馆	E 邮电局
B 电器商店		H　肯德基
C 电影院	F 食品商店	G 新潮衣店

生词　　　New words

局	jú	office	商	shāng	business, commerce
器	qì	appliance	店	diàn	shop
品	pǐn	product			

☑ Exercise 2

1 Is D a cinema or a restaurant?　　　　_____
2 Do you go to B or E to post a letter?　　_____
3 Where do you go to buy clothes?　　　　_____
4 Which is the bank?　　　　　　　　　_____
5 Would you buy a Cornetto or
  Kentucky Fried Chicken at H?　　　　_____
6 Where do you go to buy food?　　　　　_____

☑ Exercise 3

You are surprised to see how many brand names commonly found in the
West you can see in the shopping mall. In the next exercise there are five
brand names in Chinese characters. Give the English equivalent for each
of them. Which is the odd one out? (We've given you some of the *pinyin*
to help you.)

kē ní kǎ　*kěn dé jī*　*bèi kè*　　*chūn lán*　　*kě ài duō*
a) 柯尼卡　b) 肯德基　c) 贝克啤酒　d) 春兰冰箱　e) 可爱多
a) _____　b) _____　c) _____　d) _____　e) _____

The odd one out is: _____.

If you're finding this difficult, the photos overleaf may assist you:

a)

b)

c)

d)

e)

☑ Exercise 4

A Chinese friend with a car has picked you up at the shopping mall to take you to a beauty spot outside Beijing but first he has to fill up with petrol. There are building works going on at the petrol station and a large notice reads 24 小时.

Does this mean   a) Closed for 24 hours   or   b) Open 24 hours?

☑ Exercise 5

Your friend comes to a large intersection. He is a wonderful man but tends to be a little stingy. Will he take the left fork a) or the right b)? ____

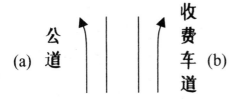

Which one would normally be the better road? ____

☑ Exercise 6

You get back pretty late, happy but tired, and decide to have a relaxing morning the next day by having a late breakfast in your room. Unfortunately you've only been left the Chinese Breakfast Room Service card (below and overleaf) to hang on your door. You decide to give it a go. You work out that there are four different types of breakfast. Can you list them in English in the order they appear on the card?

(a) _____   (c) _____
(b) _____   (d) _____

贵宾姓名: _____
人　　数: _____
签　　名: _____
房间号码: _____
日　　期: _____

所需服务时间
☐ 6:00 – 6:30　☐ 6:30 – 7:00　☐ 7:00 – 7:30　☐ 7:30 – 8:00
☐ 8:00 – 8:30　☐ 8:30 – 9:00　☐ 9:00 – 9:30　☐ 9:30 – 10:00

国际特式早餐   80.00

各式果汁任选
☐ 橙汁　　　　　　☐ 蜜瓜汁　　　　　☐ 西瓜汁
扒芝士火腿多士
蛋花热麦片
新鲜提子苹果碟
饮料任选
☐ 咖啡　　　　　　☐ 茶

美式早餐   78.00

各式冰冻果汁任选
☐ 橙汁　　　　　　☐ 西柚汁　　　　　☐ 菠萝汁
☐ 提子汁　　　　　☐ 苹果汁　　　　　☐ 蕃茄汁
农场鲜鸡蛋两只任选
☐ 炒　　　　　　　☐ 煎双面蛋　　　　☐ 煎
☐ 波　　　　　　　☐ 焓......分钟
配
☐ 火腿　　　　　　☐ 烟肉　　　　　　☐ 香肠
特式包点两件
☐ 牛角包　　　　　☐ 丹麦包　　　　　☐ 多士
☐ 麦菲　　　　　　☐ 早餐包
新鲜水果伴酸奶
饮料任选
☐ 咖啡　　　　　　☐ 茶

欧陆式早餐   59.00

各式冰冻果汁任选
☐ 橙汁　　　　　　☐ 西柚汁　　　　　☐ 菠萝汁
☐ 提子汁　　　　　☐ 苹果汁　　　　　☐ 蕃茄汁
特式包点两件
☐ 牛角包　　　　　☐ 丹麦包　　　　　☐ 多士
☐ 麦菲　　　　　　☐ 早餐包
选择其中一款
☐ 酸奶　　　　　　☐ 鲜果碟
饮料任选
☐ 咖啡　　　　　　☐ 茶

中式早餐   63.00

瑶柱、白果白粥
脯汁蒸肠粉
选择其中一款
☐ 炸油条　　　　　☐ 叉烧包
中国茶

所有价格另加 15%服务费

(e) What do the last two characters in each category mean?

(f) What is the one character that is common to all four categories in addition to 早餐?

(g) What does it mean (have a guess)?

(h) What are you asked to do in the first five lines at the top of the card? Please fill them in. Today is 10 August.

☑ Exercise 7

You decide to go for the second category at 78.00￥. You realise that where there is a line of characters and then a series of boxes underneath that you are probably expected to tick *one* of the boxes. You do this and hang the notice outside your door. The next morning your breakfast tray has on it: apple juice, two over easy (done on both sides) fried eggs, served with ham, two slices of toast, fresh fruit yoghurt and a pot of coffee.

(i) Which boxes did you tick? (Go back and tick what you ordered.)
(j) What did you get without having to tick a box for it?
(k) Write it out in Chinese characters too.
(l) Identify the characters for service charge and write them out.
(m) How much does the service charge add to your bill?

☑ Exercise 8

After a leisurely breakfast you decide to fill in the guest questionnaire. In the Food and Beverage section you tick good for the Cantonese restaurant, very good for the Sichuan restaurant and fair for Room Service (the eggs were hard). Which columns do you tick?

	很好	好	一般	差
广东餐厅				
四川餐厅				
送餐服务				

☑ Exercise 9

You also need to reconfirm your flight to Shanghai. On the form which
follows, the English translations have been deleted. Can you put them
back in (you will have to best guess a few of them!)? Oh, and fill out the
form in Chinese will you?!

Flight Confirmation Request	航班确认申请	
姓 _____	名 _____	房号 _____
航空公司 _____	离开日期 _____	护照号码 _____
航班号 _____	起飞时间 _____	
目的地 _____		
备注 _____		
_____		
日期 _____	客人签名 _____	接收人 _____

☑ Exercise 10

You now have to book a hotel in Shanghai. You have been given two lists
of possibles, one in Chinese and one in English but they are not in the
same order. Can you match the two? The Chinese list reads:

1 城市酒店 (上海)　　　　_____
2 上海日航饭店　　　　　_____
3 上海扬子江大酒店　　　_____
4 花園飯店 (上海)　　　　_____
5 广东国际大酒店　　　　_____
6 上海国际贵都大饭店　　_____

The English list reads:

(a) Garden Hotel Shanghai
(b) hotel Equatorial
(c) hotel Nikko Shanghai
(d) GITIC Plaza Hotel
(e) City Hotel Shanghai
(f) Yangtze New World Hotel

One of the hotels is not even in Shanghai! Your friend must have made a mistake. Which one is it? _____

1)

2)

3)
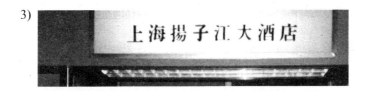

4)

5)

广东国际大酒店

6)

上海国际贵都大饭店

☑ Exercise 11

Look at the hotel names in Chinese more closely:

  i) Do they all use the same word for hotel?   Yes/No.
 ii) Which hotels put the character for 'big' in front of the word 'hotel'?
     _____
iii) In 花园飯店, are the characters written in full form or simplified
     characters? _____
 iv) Where does the word Shanghai appear in the Chinese version of
     hotel nikko Shanghai? _____
  v) In which other hotel signs does the same thing happen? _____
 vi) For which two hotels does the word 'Shanghai' appear in brackets?
     _____
vii) For which two hotels does the word 'Shanghai' appear in the Chinese
     but not in the English?

☑ Exercise 12

You have just remembered you need to send off an urgent letter to a
business acquaintance who is on holiday without a phone or fax. You
write the letter quickly and find an envelope on your desk.

```
┌─────────────────────────────────────────────────────────┐
│ ┌┬┬┬┬┐                                          贴 邮    │
│ └┴┴┴┴┘                                          票 处    │
│                                                          │
│          收件人姓名及地址                                 │
│          _____                          │
│                                                          │
│              _____                      │
│                                                          │
│          寄件人姓名及地址                                 │
│              _____                      │
│  航 空                                                    │
│              _____                      │
│                                          ┌┬┬┬┬┐          │
└──────────────────────────────────────────┴┴┴┴┴┘─────────┘
```

a) What do you think 航空 means? (cf. radical 舟)
b) Identify the two characters for postage stamp(s) by circling them.
   (贴邮票处 means 'stick stamp place'. cf. 'post office' in Exercise 2.)
c) You know 姓名 means 'name' and 地址 means 'address'. What do
   you think 及 means?
d) 收 means to 'receive'. What do you think 寄 means?
e) Write down the characters for 'sender' and 'recipient'.

8 | UNIT 8
Entertainment

After a busy day, you decide to see a Chinese film. At the local cinema, you see three films are on show that evening.

红楼
电影院

今、明日电影	
《大上海》	今晚七点、九点十分（客满）
《南方来信》	今晚八点一刻，明天上午十点半
《红河谷》	今晚九点二十，明晚六点四十五

红 *hóng* red 　 谷 *gǔ* valley

Exercise 1

Please answer the questions in Chinese.

a) What is the name of the cinema? _____

b) Which show is sold out? _____

c) It's nearly 8 o'clock. What is the next film available? _____

d) What films are showing tomorrow? _____

Cultural tip: seating in Chinese cinemas, theatre, etc.

All the even seat numbers are grouped together on one side and all the uneven ones on the other. Only seat numbers 2 and 1 are next to each other sequentially. This means that when you go into a Chinese cinema for example, you need to check whether your seat numbers are even or odd. If they are even you will need to follow the sign for 双号 *shuānghào* seats and if odd the signs for 单号 *dānhào* seats. It is obviously important to understand the way the seating is organised if ever you are buying seats yourself and to know that 楼上 *lóushàng* means 'upstairs' and 楼下 *lóuxià* 'downstairs'.

☑ Exercise 2

You are going to see a show and your ticket looks like this:

红楼电影院	电影票
六月二十日	楼上
晚七点四十五分	九排十八号

1 Will you be sitting upstairs or downstairs? _____
2 Which entrance do you go to? (i.e. odd or even numbers) _____
3 What time will the show start? _____
4 What is the date of the show? _____

☑ Exercise 3

You are staying at 北京饭店. Look at the bus stop board.

西<————————>东

人山天宝西儿明北大东中
民东地玉湖童海京同方山
公北市大路乐商饭路医路
园路场街 园城店 院

Now decide first which direction and then how many stops you should take before you:

a) get to the People's Park. _____
b) get to the Children's Amusement Park. _____
c) get to the Tiandi (Heaven and Earth) Market. _____
d) get to the Oriental (East) Hospital. _____

Exercise 4

Look at the following posters and answer the questions below. (The questions can refer to any of the posters.)

A 英国教育展 时间: 六月九日 - 六月十七日 地点: 北京大学 免费入场	B 英文图书展销会 时间: 五月七日至五月十八日 地点: 星星书店 （学院路1号） 欢迎光临
C 法国印象派画展 时间: 五月十四日 - 五月二十日 地点: 中国美术馆 票价: 20元	D 日本电器产品展销会 时间: 六月二十四日至七月九日 地点: 北京展览馆 票价: 10元

1 Where is the British Education Exhibition taking place?
2 How much does it cost to go the French Impressionist Exhibition?
3 What is on sale at the Japanese Fair?
4 Books in which language are being exhibited at the Star Bookshop?
5 How many days is the French Impressionist Exhibition on for?
6 Which two exhibitions are free? (cf. Unit 7, Exercise 1)
7 Which exhibition is on for the longest?

Exercise 5

A fairly standard form can be seen overleaf. Try and work out what information you are being asked for. (We have added letters for ease of reference.)

(a) 姓名:	(b) 中文:	(c) 英文:
(d) 性别:	(e) 出生年月: 年 月 日	
(f) 现住址:		
(g) 电话:		
(h) 工作单位:		

(a) _____   (b) _____   (c) _____   (d) _____

(e) _____   (f) _____   (g) _____   (h) _____

Cultural tip

The measurements used in China are different from those used in the UK. The following is a table of measurements:

1 尺 (*chǐ*)	= 1.094 英尺 (*yīngchǐ*) foot
1 英尺	= 0.305 米 (*mǐ*) metre
1 米	= 1.094 码 (*mǎ*) yard
1 码	= 0.914 米
1 公里 (*gōnglǐ*)	= 0.621 英里 (*yīnglǐ*) mile
1 英里	= 1.609 公里 kilometre
1 斤* (*jīn*)	= 1.102 磅 (*bàng*) pound
1 磅	= 0.454 公斤 kilogram

* 斤 is a radical in its own right.

☑ Exercise 6

Prepare a note to give to a taxi driver, telling him where you want to go. You can start the note with 我要去 which means 'I want to go to', although this is not essential. For example: I want to go to Number 12 Peace Road – 我要去和平路12号.

a) 8 West Lake Road   _____

b) The Oriental Hotel   _____

c) The Children's Amusement Park   _____

d) The People's Park   _____

☑ Exercise 7

Give the stroke order of the following characters and put the radical in the brackets after each one.

饭 ＿ ＿ ＿ ＿ ＿ ＿ ＿ ( )
楼 ＿ ＿ ＿ ＿ ＿ ＿ ＿ ＿ ＿ ＿ ＿ ＿ ＿ ＿ ( )
河 ＿ ＿ ＿ ＿ ＿ ＿ ＿ ＿ ( )
院 ＿ ＿ ＿ ＿ ＿ ＿ ＿ ＿ ＿ ( )
场 ＿ ＿ ＿ ＿ ＿ ＿ ( )

You are now on your way to the airport. First of all you have to pay the airport tax.

How much is it? Yes, 50￥, but have you noticed that 50 is not written as 五十 but as 伍拾? This is because numbers on tickets, coupons and bank notes, on forms in banks and post offices, etc. are written differently from the (simple) ones you learnt in Unit 4. This is to prevent forgeries or misunderstandings. (It would be easy, for instance, to make 一 into 三.) The Chinese call this 大写 (big write), so 伍 is 五字的大写 (the character 五 written big).

Here are the two lists of numbers for you to compare:

Ordinary numbers   一 二 三 四 五 六 七 八 九 十
'Complex' numbers   壹 贰 叁 肆 伍 陆 柒 捌 玖 拾

Three examples of bank notes which all use the 'complex' numbers follow. There are ten 角 (*jiǎo*) in one 圆 (*yuán*) (which is also written in the full form). 元 (*yuán*) is the simplified form used in daily life).

☑ Exercise 8

Your business in 上海 is finished and you are flying from 上海 to pick up your flight in 香港. Here is your boarding card (登机牌).

CAAC	中国民航		登机牌	
航班号	日期	时间	目的地	登机门
5359	六月七日	九点四十	上海	后门

a) Is the destination correct? _____

b) What is the date and time of your flight? _____

c) Which door are you told to take, the front door or the rear one?
_____

You are given the menu for the meal you will be served on the flight. It is shown in both simplified and full characters. The full-character version was the original and is on the right.

轻膳	輕膳
上海 -- 香港	上海 -- 香港
青瓜沙律	青瓜沙律
*	*
韩式牛骨排	韓式牛骨排
白饭	白飯
中式鲜蔬	中式鮮蔬
或	或
咖哩烩鸡	咖哩燴雞
野米饭	野米飯
*	*
鲜果	鮮菓
*	*
面包、牛油	麵包、牛油
*	*
红茶、日本绿茶、中国茶	紅茶、日本綠茶、中國茶
咖啡	咖啡

☑ Exercise 9

Now answer the following questions based on the menu above:

a) What do the characters 香港 mean? _____

b) Is rice served with the meal? _____

c) Is beef on the menu? _____

d) You have two choices of main meal which are joined by the character for 'or'. Which is it? _____

e) What is the dessert? _____

f) What hot drinks can you choose from after the meal? (红 *hóng* = red; 绿 *lü* = green) _____ _____ _____ _____

You are now on your flight back to London (伦敦). The services offered by the cabin crew are shown in the card:

鸡尾酒
*
晚餐
*
免税精品销售
*

小吃
鸡味即食面
三文治
阁下如需享用以上各款小吃，请向机舱服务员索取
*

免税精品销售
请注意，此项服务于航机抵达目的地之两小时前停止。
*

热毛巾及果汁
*

香
港
‖
伦
敦

🍴 Exercise 10

Please answer the following questions (some good guesswork is required!):

a) Is duty free mentioned? How many times?

b) When does in-flight shopping stop?

c) Circle the characters for 'attendant'.

d) Which comes first on the menu, breakfast or dinner?

e) What do you think 小吃 are? _____

f) What is a 三文治 (*sān wén zhì*) (say the whole word aloud and you should be able to guess it correctly)? _____

g) What do you get with your wake-up towel? _____

Cultural tip

In the People's Republic of China there are four municipal cities (Beijing, Shanghai, Tianjin and Chongqing), 22 provinces (excluding Taiwan), five autonomous regions (including Tibet) and two special administrative regions (Hong Kong and Macao).

Each has a single character as its short form. Here are some examples:

北京	*Běijīng*	京		四川	*Sìchuān*	川	
上海	*Shànghǎi*	沪	*hù*	广东	*Guǎngdōng*	粤	*yuè*
天津	*Tiānjīn*	津		香港	*Xiānggǎng*	港	
山东	*Shāndōng*	鲁	*lǔ*	青海	*Qīnghǎi*	青	
湖南	*Húnán*	湘	*xiāng*	西藏	*Xīzàng*	藏	

This is used in a number of situations. Some of the railway lines and motorways are named after the two cities or provinces which the railways or motorways have connected. For example, 京沪线 (线 *xiàn* rail line), 京津公路 (公路 *gōnglù* highway, an A road), 青藏公路 etc. The regional styles of opera are thus termed 京剧 (剧 *jù* drama), 沪剧, 川剧. Types of cuisine are also called 川菜, 粤菜 etc.

9 | UNIT 9
The weather

This chapter will provide you with general information on the weather and how to write notes and postcards in Chinese. It will also include a section on calligraphy and the different styles of writing Chinese characters which have always been highly prized by the Chinese.

You have been back in Britain for four months now and feel very proud of the postcard you have just written to your Chinese friend for his birthday: you feel your writing has made real progress!

大明，

　　你好!

　　我回英国已经六个月了，工作常常很忙，可是我很高兴。
我很想你! 下个月是你的生日, 祝你:

　　生日快乐! 身体健康! 工作愉快! 万事如意!

　　　　　　　　　　　　你的朋友

　　　　　　　　　　　　海伦

　　　　　　　　　　　　九月十八日

生词	*Shēngcí*	New words
回	*huí*	return
已经	*yǐjīng*	already
工作	*gōngzuò*	(to) work
常常	*chángcháng*	often
忙	*máng*	busy
可是	*kěshì*	but
高兴	*gāoxìng*	happy
想	*xiǎng*	to miss (somebody); to think (of)
生日	*shēngrì*	birthday
祝	*zhù*	to wish

快乐	*kuàilè*	happy, pleasant
身体	*shēntǐ*	body, health
健康	*jiànkāng*	healthy
万事	*wànshì*	10,000 matters
如意	*rúyì*	as one wishes
朋友	*péngyou*	friend

The Chinese often finish their letters by using phrases like:

祝你
	Literal translation	
走运!	Walk lucky	Good luck!
生日快乐!	Birthday happy	Happy birthday!
一路平安!	All the way peace	Bon voyage!
身体健康!	Body healthy	Good health!
工作愉快!	Work happy	Happiness in your work!
万事如意!	10,000 things as wish	May everything turn out exactly as you would wish it!

Common greetings at festivals are:

祝你
新年快乐!	新 new	年 year	Happy New Year!
春节快乐!	春 spring	节 festival	Happy (Chinese) New Year!
情人节快乐!	情 affection	情人 lover	Happy Valentine's Day!
复活节快乐!	复 again	活 living	Happy Easter!
圣诞节快乐!	圣 holy	诞 birth	Happy Christmas!

Cultural tip

The Chinese seem to have a passion for numbers. Many idioms have numbers in them. 万事如意 is one of them. 万 is a particularly favoured word in Chinese culture. Unlike in English where 10,000 means ten thousand, the Chinese has a term 万 for it, and it represented and still represents a very large number. While in English one may wish someone (or a cause) a long life by saying 'Long live XX', the Chinese equivalent is to wish someone or something to live 万岁 *wàn suì* '10,000 years'. Therefore, 万岁 was used to address or greet emperors. Understandably, it was also used for Mao Zedong, the late Chinese leader. His supporters used to wave his little red book and shout: '毛主席万岁、万万岁!' '*Máo zhǔxí* wàn suì、wàn wàn suì!*' (主席 *zhǔxí* chairman).

Here are some other commonly used idioms with numbers in them:

Literal meaning

一心一意	one heart one mind
三心二意	three hearts and two minds
一心二用	one heart two uses
一国两制	one country two systems
三言两语	three words and two speeches
七上八下	seven ups and eight downs
百年大计	100 years big plan
千山万水	1,000 mountains and 10,000 waters
千家万户	1,000 families and 10,000 household(s)
千言万语	1,000 words and 10,000 speeches

☑ Exercise 1

Here are the 'proper' translations for the idioms above but they are not in the same order. Can you match them up?

a) not giving undivided attention to something
b) to be in two minds
c) whole-hearted(ness); with undivided attention
d) one country two systems
e) to be in a state of anxiety and nervousness
f) (of speech) brief
g) (covering) a vast area of land
h) every family and household
i) (there is) a great deal to express
j) a project of vital and far-reading importance

☑ Exercise 2

We feel that we can't let you finish this book without practising your weather vocabulary! Here is the weather forecast 天气预报 *tiānqì yùbào* for tomorrow in a Chinese newspaper. See if you are able to answer the questions after it.

> ＜人民日报＞　　　四月二十七日　星期六
>
> 　　　　　　　天气预报
> 今天白天晴　　　　　今天晚上阴，有小雨
> 风向: 南风　　　　　风向: 西北
> 风力: 一、二级　　　风力: 四、五级
> 最高气温20 °C　　　最低气温8 °C

1 When will the weather be fine today?
2 What direction will the wind be coming from:
   a) during the day?　　　b) during the night?
3 Will the wind be stronger in the evening or during the day?
4 When will it rain?
5 What is tomorrow's date?

报上说今天不会下雨
But the paper said it wouldn't rain today.

☑ Exercise 3

Read the following postcards and answer the questions after them. (The
questions can refer to any of the postcards.)

> 小王:
>
> 你好!
> 我们的会谈很成功，我认识了很多新朋友。
> 我现在住在和平饭店，这里的饭菜都很好吃。
>
> 祝你春节快乐!
> 　　　　　　　你的朋友 李和平
> 　　　　　　　九八年一月十五日

美：

你好！南京天气很不好，天天下雨。我很想你。
祝你情人节快乐！爱你！

大海
二月六日

小明：

你好！
北京真好。每天天气都很好，不冷不热。昨天我去了人民
大会堂。我明天去西安。

祝你圣诞节快乐！

你的朋友   马天民
二〇〇〇年十二月七号

---

1 Which hotel was Li Heping staying in?
2 What was the food like at Li Heping's hotel?
3 Which city was Ma Tianmin staying in?
4 Where did he go yesterday?
5 Where was the weather good?
6 Where did it rain?
7 Why was Dahai writing to Mei?
8 Where is Ma Tianmin going tomorrow?
9 When did Li Heping write to Xiao Wang?

Cultural tip

Traditionally, Chinese writing was done from right to left and from
top to bottom. This tradition has been largely kept in Hong Kong and
Taiwan where newspaper articles as well as books are still mostly
printed vertically. The following is an illustration.

平衡集

英語

九七年前，人們對回歸祖國以後有很大假設或者看法，到了今天發覺並不一一實現，例如九七年之後此地人們不再覺得要學好英語。

近十年間，香港的大學生英語水準下降是人所周知的事，法律學生自不例外，於是早幾年前有些人覺得香港法庭變成中文世界的日子即將來臨，英語好不好也不打緊了，法庭遲早全用中文聆訊，政治正確最重要。

那知道過了九七，不止香港人仍在學英語，國內的人更多在學英語，根據統計數字，此刻中國國內在學英語的學生比在美國說英語的美國人還要多。

Calligraphy

Even today, the art of calligraphy (the writing of Chinese characters as an art form) is highly regarded in China and many educated Chinese will hang scrolls of characters, beautifully mounted, on their walls, just as we would hang a picture by, say, Turner or Picasso. Calligraphers all have their own individual styles and, of course, their admirers and critics, just as painters do. (As calligraphy is an art with its roots in the ancient past, these scrolls are always written in the traditional way from top to bottom and usually in their full form which is visually more pleasing.) Look at the examples.

北宋　米芾　多景楼帖冊
Album of Calligraphy in
Duo Jing Lou (detail)
running script
by Mi Fu · Northern Song

元　赵孟頫　十札卷
Ten Letters Running Script (detail)
by Zhao Mengfu · Yuan

元　倪瓒　渔庄秋霁图轴
Fishing Village in the Clear
Autumn Day
by Ni Zan · Yuan

明　沈周
仿大痴山水图轴
Landscape after Da Chi
by Shen Zhou · Ming

Does the following couplet look familiar?

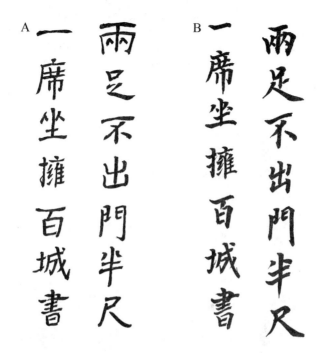

Yes, it is on the cover of this book! A is written in the same style as on the cover whereas B is written in a different style.

Here they are again in their printed form in both full and simplified characters, with the full form on the left. The new words and translation follow after. Would you be surprised if we tell you that out of the fourteen characters, you have already come across twelve?!

兩足不出門半尺
一席坐擁百城書

两足不出门半尺
一席坐拥百城书

生词   *Shēngcí*   New words

席	*xí*	mat, seat (cf. 主席 chairman)
拥	*yōng*	to possess (扌 hand radical)
城	*chéng*	town, city (土 earth radical)

两	足	不	出	门	半	尺
two	foot	not	out	door	half	foot (length)

一	席	坐	拥	百	城	书
one	seat	sit	have	hundred	town	book

(I) do not (have to) step out of the door half a foot,
(yet I) sit surrounded by books from a hundred towns.

And what about the following eight characters which run from right to left and top to bottom? You will find them on the cover, too!

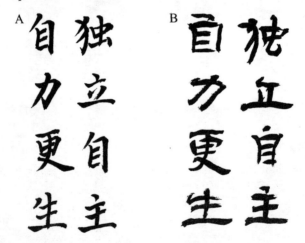

独立自主   to be independent and self-reliant
自力更生   to rely on one's own strength to regenerate

生词   *Shēngcí*   New words

独	*dú*	independent, alone
立	*lì*	to stand (*a radical*)
自	*zì*	self (*a radical*)
主	*zhǔ*	to take the initiative
更	*gēng*	to change, to replace

☑ **Exercise 4**

Test your recognition of 'stylised' characters. You might find this hard at first. Look at the sign and answer the following questions.

1 Complete the characters for 'snack' and 'tea'   中西＿＿餐、＿＿座
2 Write out the character for Conference (Room) ＿＿＿ ＿＿＿ 厅
3 Rewrite the character after 大 in its 'normal' form. ＿＿＿
4 What do the last four characters mean? ＿＿＿＿＿＿＿

Seals

Seals are used for institutional as well as individual purposes such as signatures on documents (bank or PO deposits) and on paintings or scrolls.

(Go back and look at the paintings and examples of calligraphy in this unit.) Just like calligraphy, seals are viewed as an art form as they involve both design and calligraphy. The following three examples are from different dynasties.

(i) Western Han 西汉   (ii) Western Jin 西晋   (iii) Qing 清
    (206BC–23AD)   (265–316AD)   (1644–1911)

MAIN TEST

☑ Exercise 1

Amend the word order in each of the following sentences and then put them in the correct sequence.

1 我休息中午。
2 我十一点睡觉晚上。
3 我四点下午去喝茶。
4 我起床七点一刻早上。   The correct sequence is ___ ___ ___ ___

☑ Exercise 2

Write the address in Chinese on the envelope to your pen pal.

- Mr Wang Mingshan*   _____
- 9 East Lake Road   _____
- International University   _____
- Nanjing, China   _____

[* where *ming* is bright, and *shān* is mountain.]

(Remember that the Chinese write the bigger place (i.e. the country) first and the individual person last.)

✔ Exercise 3

Leave a notice using the following form at the reception counter of the hotel you are staying in. The notice is intended for a Chinese friend who does not read any English, telling her your whereabouts during the day in case she comes to visit you. Write in Chinese and include the following information:

Today's date is 6 September.
You will be at the Oriental University.
From 8.30am to 4.30pm.
Comments: You will return to the hotel at 5pm.
Your room number is 526 and your name is Helen/David King.

Where are you? 你在哪里?

Date 日期 _____

I will be at 我将在 _____

From   am/pm to   am/pm

从 _____ 上午/下午至 _____ 上午/下午

Comments 要求 _____

_____

Name 姓名 _____ Room No. 房号 _____

Signature 签名 _____

Peace Hotel   西安

Xi'an   和平宾馆

✔ Exercise 4

Write a postcard in Chinese characters to your Chinese friend in Beijing saying that you really like Shanghai. The weather is sunny but often windy. Tell her you are going by train to Nanjing. You are going back to your friend's in Beijing on 5 March. Tell her you miss her. (Refer back to Unit 6, Exercise 15 for some help with the vocabulary.)

✔ Exercise 5

Look at the next few signs and see if you can give the answers for each of them.

A
百香咖啡厅
位于一楼
24小时营业

1 What is Pepper's Chinese name? Please write it out in characters.

_____

2 Is Pepper's a restaurant?　　_____
3 Where is it situated?　　　　_____
4 What are its opening hours?　_____

B
艺苑酒廊
位于二楼
早晨11:00至凌晨01:00营业

1 Where is it in the hotel?
2 What are its opening hours?

C
香怡阁
正宗粤式烹饪
位于三楼
午餐:　11:30–14:00
晚餐:　17:30–22:30

1 What sort of food does it serve? (Go back and look at the Cultural tip on page 85.)

2 Where is it located?
3 Does it serve breakfast?

D

罗马意大利餐厅
正宗意大利风味
位于三楼
晚餐: 17:30–22:30

1 What kind of restaurant is it? (see names of countries in Unit 5)
2 Where is it situated?
3 What meals does it serve?

✔ Exercise 6

Look carefully at the photos that follow.

1 What do you think is happening at the booth besides the advertising of
   Beck's beer?

2 Is the following sign advertising ice-cream, freezers or furniture?

3 Which city was the following photo taken in? Which department put up the notice? (Look up unfamiliar characters in your dictionary.)

☑ Exercise 7

Which platform would you go to if you wanted to go to the following cities: Beijing (   ), Xi'an (   ), Nanjing (   ), Shanghai (   )? Put the correct platform number in the brackets after each city.

车次	开往	时间	站台
123	南京	12点05分	12
214	西安	12点17分	4
14	上海	13点26分	6
27	北京	14点30分	9

(cf. 服务台 in Unit 5.)

Exercise 8

The next two signs are strictly for fun. Can you spot the two characters for 'delicious' in (a)? Try and write them out. ___ ___

(a)

The proper translation for (a) would be something like this:

Chewing gum is delicious   口香糖好吃
Dirty stains are difficult to get rid of   污渍难除
Please do not spit it out at random   请君莫乱吐
Treasure cultural relics   珍惜文物

The photograph in Exercise 8(a) is actually written in the form of a quatrain with lines 2, 3 and 4 rhyming!

(b)

芳草有情　盼您有义
So fragrant the lawn
So warm-hearted as you

Can you spot the character for 'grass' in (b)? It is ___. The sign actually means:

The fragrant grass has feelings
It hopes that you have righteousness (i.e. to look after it).
(It looks at you with meaning!)

10 UNIT 10
How to use a Chinese–English dictionary

In this unit we explain how to use a Chinese–English dictionary and give you some information on Chinese word-processing. We finish by explaining a little about Chinese idioms, which are so popular in both the written and spoken language.

Using a Chinese–English dictionary

Most of the dictionaries you will have access to, use *pinyin* to list the characters in alphabetical order according to their pronunciation and tone. This is only of use if you know how a particular character is pronounced, otherwise you will have to look it up using the radical. (There are other systems but this is the most common and the most straightforward at this stage.) Having identified the radical (not always so easy but refer to the table of radicals that follows for help) and counted up the number of strokes it has, you look for it in the radical index at the front of the dictionary.

We have included the radical index from a popular dictionary on p. 105 (汉英词典 *A Chinese–English Dictionary*). It may prove useful to you as a reference. The number to the left of the radical indicates the order in which it appears.

Radicals are arranged under sub-headings according to the number of strokes they have (一画 *yī huà* one stroke, 二画 *èr huà* two strokes, 三画 *sān huà* three strokes . . . usually up to twelve and over, 十二画以上 *shí'èr huà yǐshàng*). Each radical has a number assigned to it which may vary slightly from dictionary to dictionary so don't automatically assume it's the same. Having found which number radical it is (the number may be to the left or to the right of the radical itself), look it up in the character index proper which immediately follows and which lists each radical in the order in which it appears in the radical index. Under each radical are listed all the characters which have that radical in common and they in turn are listed under the same sub-headings as in the radical index, 一画、二画 ... 十八画以上, i.e. the number of strokes the character has when the radical has been taken away.

Radicals with comparatively few characters assigned to them may not list each sub-heading individually but may sometimes group a few of them together, e.g. 六至八画 *liù zhì bā huà* six to eight strokes, 九至十一画 nine to eleven strokes, etc.

Thus 情 *qíng* (emotions) is listed under the heart radical 忄, under the sub-heading eight strokes 八画, and will come *after* 恨 *hèn* (hate; to hate) which comes under the sub-heading six strokes 六画, which in turn will come after 怕 *pà* (to fear) listed under five strokes 五画. Another example is 饭 *fàn* (cooked rice; food) which will come under the food radical 饣 and be listed under the sub-heading four strokes 四画 and will precede 饱 *bǎo* (have eaten one's fill, be full) which will be listed under the sub-heading five strokes 五画. We hope you have got the idea!

Let's assume you have found the character you were looking for in the index (检字表). Next to it will either be a page number or the *pinyin* and tone mark for it, either of which will enable you to look it up in the main body of the dictionary.

Remember that characters with the same pronunciation are listed with those in the first tone (indicated by ‾) first, then those in the second tone (indicated by ´), which in turn precede those in the third (ˇ) and fourth (`) tones respectively. It sounds hard work but it's not as bad as it looks once you get the hang of it and it can be very satisfying! It is reckoned that there are around 4,000 characters in daily use of which approximately 2,000 are needed to get a general idea of what is going on in a newspaper.

Now try looking up three different characters in the dictionary. (We've printed the relevant pages for you.)

1) 贺   2) 物   3) 氧

Step 1   Identify the radical and find it in the radical index.

Step 2   Find the radical in the character index.

Step 3   Count up the number of strokes in the character once you have taken the radical away.

Step 4   Look under the sub-heading with the corresponding number of strokes and find your character.

Step 5   Go to the page indicated and locate the character again. Bingo!

部 首 检 字
Radical Index

（一）部首目录

部首左边的号码表示部首的次序

一　画	35 又	70 ヨ(彐彑)	105 中	140 业	175 缶	209 金
1 、	36 廴	71 弓	106 贝	141 目	176 耒	九　画
2 一	37 厶	72 己(已)	107 见	142 田	177 舌	210 鱼
3 丨	38 凵	73 女	108 父	143 由	178 竹(⺮)	211 音
4 丿	39 匕	74 子(孑)	109 气	144 申	179 臼	212 革
5 乛	三　画	75 马	110 牛(牜)	145 罒	180 自	213 韭
6 亅	40 氵	76 幺	111 手	146 皿	181 血	214 骨
7 乙(乛乚)	41 忄	77 纟(糸)	112 毛	147 钅	182 舟	215 香
二　画	42 丬(爿)	78 巛	113 攵	148 矢	183 羽	216 鬼
8 冫	43 亡	79 小(⺌)	114 片	149 禾	184 艮(艮)	217 食
9 亠	44 广	四　画	115 斤	150 白	七　画	十　画
10 讠	45 宀	80 灬	116 爪(爫)	六　画	185 言	218 高
11 二	46 门	81 心	117 尺	151 瓜	186 辛	219 鬲
12 十	47 辶	82 斗	118 月	152 鸟	187 辰	220 髟
13 厂	48 工	83 火	119 殳	153 皮	188 麦	十一画
14 ナ	49 土(士)	84 文	120 欠	154 癶	189 走	221 麻
15 匚	50 廾	85 方	121 风	155 矛	190 赤	222 鹿
16 卜(⺊)	51 艹	86 户	122 氏	156 疋	191 豆	十二画
17 刂	52 大	87 礻	123 比	157 羊(⺷羋)	192 束	223 黑
18 冖	53 尢	88 王	124 聿	158 关	193 酉	十三画
19 冂	54 寸	89 主	125 水	159 米	194 豕	224 鼓
20 𠂉	55 扌	90 天(夭)	五　画	160 齐	195 里	225 鼠
21 亻	56 弋	91 韦	126 立	161 衣	196 足	十四画
22 𠆢	57 巾	92 耂	127 疒	162 亦(亦)	197 釆	226 鼻
23 人(入)	58 口	93 廿(卅)	128 穴	163 耳	198 豸	227 余类
24 八(丷)	59 囗	94 木	129 衤	164 臣	199 谷	
25 乂	60 山	95 不	130 夫	165 戋	200 身	
26 勹	61 彳	96 犬	131 玉	166 西(覀)	201 角	
27 刀(⺈)	62 彡	97 歹	132 示	167 束	八　画	
28 力	63 夕	98 瓦	133 去	168 亚	202 青	
29 儿	64 夂	99 牙	134 艹	169 而	203 其	
30 几(凡)	65 丸	100 车	135 甘	170 页	204 雨	
31 マ	66 尸	101 戈	136 石	171 至	205 非	
32 卩	67 屮	102 止	137 龙	172 光	206 齿	
33 阝(在左)	68 飞	103 日	138 戊	173 虍	207 黾	
34 阝(在右)	69 犭	104 曰	139 母	174 虫	208 隹	

阖 hé 〈书〉① entire; whole: ～城 the whole town/ ～家 the whole family ② shut; close: ～户 close the door

貉 hé racoon dog
另见 háo

翮 hé ① shaft of a feather; quill ② wing (of a bird): 振～高飞 flap the wings and soar high into the sky

hè

吓 hè ① threaten; intimidate ② 〈叹〉〔表示不满〕: ～怎么能干这种事呢? Tut-tut, how could you do that?
另见 xià

和 hè ① join in the singing: 一唱百～。When one starts singing, all the others join in. ② compose a poem in reply: 奉～一首 write a poem in reply (to one sent by a friend, etc., using the same rhyme sequence)
另见 hé; huó; huò

贺 hè ① congratulate ②(Hè) a surname
【贺词】 hècí speech (或 message) of congratulation; con-gratulations; greetings
【贺电】 hèdiàn message of congratulation; congratulatory telegram
【贺礼】 hèlǐ gift (as a token of congratulation)
【贺年】 hènián extend New Year greetings or pay a New Year call ◇ ～片 New Year card
【贺喜】 hèxǐ congratulate sb. on a happy occasion (e.g. a wedding, the birth of a child, etc.)
【贺信】 hèxìn congratulatory letter; letter of congratulation

荷 hè 〈书〉① carry on one's shoulder or back: ～锄 carry a hoe on one's shoulder/ ～枪实弹 carry a loaded rifle ② burden; responsibility: 肩负重～ shoulder heavy re-sponsibilities ③〔多用于书信〕grateful; obliged: 无任感～。I'll be very much obliged./ 请早日示复为～。An early reply will be appreciated.
另见 hé
【荷载】 hèzài load

喝 hè shout loudly: ～问 shout a question to/ 大～一声 give a loud shout
另见 hē
【喝彩】 hècǎi acclaim; cheer: 齐声～ cheer in chorus; cheer with one accord/ 博得全场～ bring the house down
【喝倒彩】 hè dàocǎi make catcalls; hoot; boo
【喝令】 hèlìng shout an order (或 command)

褐 hè ① 〈书〉coarse cloth or clothing ② brown
【褐煤】 hèméi brown coal; lignite
【褐色土】 hèsètǔ drab soil
【褐铁矿】 hètiěkuàng brown iron ore; limonite
【褐藻】 hèzǎo 〈植〉brown alga

Two Dictionary Extracts

[养尊处优] yǎngzūn-chǔyōu enjoy high position and live in ease and comfort; live in clover

氧 yǎng <化> oxygen (O)
[氧合作用] yǎnghé zuòyòng <生理> oxygenation
[氧化] yǎnghuà <化> oxidize; oxidate
◇ ~剂 oxidizer; oxidant/ ~铁 ferric oxide/ ~物 oxide/ ~焰 oxidizing flame/ ~抑制剂 oxidation retarder (或 inhibitor)/ ~作用 oxidation
[氧气] yǎngqì oxygen
◇ ~顶吹转炉 oxygen top-blown convertor/ ~炼钢 oxygen steelmaking/ ~面具 oxygen mask/ ~瓶 oxygen cylinder/ ~枪 <冶> oxygen lance/ ~帐 <医> oxygen tent
[氧乙炔吹管] yǎngyǐquē chuīguǎn <机> oxyacetylene blow-pipe

痒 yǎng itch; tickle; 浑身发~ itch all over/ 搔到~处 scratch where it itches — hit the nail on the head/ 怕~ ticklish
[痒痒] yǎngyang <口> itch; tickle; tickle: 蚊子咬得腿上直~。The mosquito bites on my leg itch terribly.

yàng

怏 yàng
[怏怏] yàngyàng disgruntled; sullen: ~不乐 unhappy about sth.; morose

恙 yàng <书> ailment; illness: 无~ in good health/ 偶染微~ feel slightly indisposed
[恙虫] yàngchóng <动> tsutsugamushi mite ◇ ~热 tsutsugamushi disease; scrub typhus

务 wù ① affair; business: 公~ official business/ 任~ task; job/ 不急之~ business requiring no immediate attention; a matter of no great urgency ② be engaged in; devote one's efforts to: ~农 be engaged in agriculture; be a farmer/ 不~正业 not engage in honest work; not attend to one's proper duties ③ must; be sure to: ~使大家明了这一点。Be sure to make this point clear to everyone./ ~请光临指导 You are cordially invited to come and give guidance.
[务必] wùbì must; be sure to: 你~在本周内去看望他一次。Be sure to go and see him before the week is out.
[务实] wùshí deal with concrete matters relating to work
[务使] wùshǐ make sure; ensure
[务须] wùxū 见"务必"
[务虚] wùxū discuss principles or ideological guidelines

芴 wù <化> fluorene

坞 wù ① a depressed place: 船~ dock/ 花~ sunken flower-bed ② <书> a fortified building; castle

物 wù ① thing; matter: 废~ waste matter/ 矿~ minerals/ 公~ public property/ 以~易~ barter/ 地大~博 vast territory and rich resources ② the outside world as distinct from oneself; other people: 待人接~ the way one gets along with people ③ content; substance: 言之无~ talk or writing devoid of substance
[物产] wùchǎn products; produce
[物故] wùgù <书> pass away; die
[物归原主] wù guī yuánzhǔ return sth. to its rightful owner

☑ Exercise 1

For each of the following characters take out the radical and then count up the number of strokes remaining. Indicate what the radical is.

Example: 星 → 5 (日)

(a) 公	(b) 期	(c) 报	(d) 场	(e) 箭
(f) 楼	(g) 电	(h) 德	(i) 拿	(j) 室
(k) 路	(l) 海	(m) 馆	(n) 旅	

☑ Exercise 2

Write a character for each of the following phonetic transcriptions so as to make a word with the character given. (You might have to check some of these in the Vocabulary at the back of the book.)

Example: 冰 *xiāng* → 冰(箱)

(a) *shàng* 午, *xià* 午   (b) 十点 *bàn*
(c) 三点一 *kè*   (d) *wǎn* 上
(e) *Fǎ* 国, *Zhōng* 国   (f) 电 *yǐng*, 电 *huà*
(g) 啤 *jiǔ*   (h) 红 *chá*
(i) 咖 *fēi*   (j) 餐 *tīng*
(k) *nán* 厕所   (l) *gōng* 共汽 *chē*, *chū* 租汽 *chēzhàn*
(m) 东 *běi*, *běi* 京   (n) 上 *hǎi*, *Hǎinán*

☑ Exercise 3

Translate the following passage into English. You will have to look up any unfamiliar characters in a Chinese–English dictionary:

近十年间, 香港的大学生英语水准下降是人所周知的事, 法律学生自不例外 ...... 哪知道过了九七,* 不止香港人仍在学英语, 国内的人更多在学英语, 原来根据统计数字, 此刻中国国内在学英语的学生比在美国说英语的美国人还要多。(Taken from the Hong Kong newspaper article on p. 91 but written in simplified characters.)

*1997 the date when Hong Kong was returned to the People's Republic of China.

Chinese word-processing

No one denies that Chinese characters are more difficult to write than English and most other languages in the world. As you have read in the previous section it is more complicated to look up a character in a Chinese dictionary than to look up an English word in an English dictionary. How about word-processing with a computer in this computer age?

The Chinese claim that they were the first to use letter press printing some 1,500 years ago. While in the West the use of a portable typewriter was quite common, hardly any Chinese even got near to a Chinese 'typewriter'. It was a clumsy machine. The typist had to select each lead character from a pool and punch it to print on a stencil, which was then used to print on paper. It was a very slow process!

Computers have changed the world. Typing, or writing in general for that matter, has been made much easier and faster. Some 20 years ago when computers became widely available in the West and transformed writing, many people, Chinese and Westerners alike, thought that Chinese writing was doomed in the computer age. How can a writing system as complicated as Chinese possibly be processed by a computer as fast and easily as English? Surprisingly, the answer is: it can! In fact, the number of Chinese word processing packages available in computer software shops is increasing rapidly.

There are, broadly speaking, two main input methods. One could be termed the phonetic input method and the other the component input method.

Phonetic input method

If you are familiar with *pinyin*, the phonetic representation of the sounds in the Chinese language, this should be straightforward. Even if you are not, you have come across it many times in this book. It is the phonetic system that we have adopted throughout. Refer also to the pronunciation guide for a fuller explanation.

Every character can be represented in *pinyin*, i.e. a representation of how it is supposed to sound. Logically, you can key in the *pinyin* of a character and the character should show up. This is the underlying principle of this input method. You may ask 'but what about tones and homonyms?' As you already know, there are four tones in the Modern Standard/Mandarin

Chinese sound system. The same *pinyin* spelling with different tones will suggest different words. Even the same *pinyin* with the same tone would suggest different words. These are called homonyms. Take the sound *qing* for example. The *Xinhua (New China) Dictionary*, the most popular pocket Chinese dictionary in China, has listed the following:

qīng 青圊清蜻鲭轻氢倾卿   *qǐng* 苘顷庼请謦

qíng 勍黥情晴氰檠擎   *qìng* 庆亲箐綮磬罄

All the characters in the same horizontal line are homonyms. When you key in *qing* in the computer, you would expect these characters to appear. You then need to select the one you want. Most *pinyin* input methods would ignore the tones and show all the characters with the same sound regardless of the tones. This is to minimise the number of keys you have to hit for a character. You will find that some of the sounds, such as *gei*, *gen* etc. have only one or two characters. Some, however, may have as many as 40 or 60 characters, such *ji*, *xi* etc. The solution to it is to list characters according to their frequency in use, unlike the dictionary where characters are arranged according to radical and the number of strokes. Therefore, when you key in *qing* on the computer for the character 晴 (sunny), the following list may appear:

1 请 2 轻 3 清 4 青 5 情 6 晴 7 氢 8 倾 9 庆 0 擎

You then key in 6 to select 晴. If you hit the ↓ arrow key, it will give you the next ten characters, and so on.

You may have noticed that some Chinese words are formed with one character, such as 好 (good) and 大 (big), while others are formed with more than one character. For example, 朋友 (friend) and 今天 (today) both have two characters. It is therefore important to be aware that Chinese characters and English words are not equivalents. While most single characters can function as independent words on their own, most words consist of two characters, and some three characters. This is not difficult to understand. As we mentioned earlier, some 4,000 characters are used in daily life and general writing. These 4,000 characters form tens of thousands of words and expressions. In this century, hardly any new Chinese characters have been created, but some tens of thousands of new words and expressions have come into the Chinese vocabulary, and more are entering without the need to increase the number of characters.

While there are many homonyms with a single sound, there are far fewer
two-character words which share exactly the same pronunciation and
tone. It is precisely because of this that the Chinese word-processing
system will allow you to type the *pinyin* of a whole word, such as *pengyou*
and *jintian* for you to get 朋友 and 今天. There are no other words in
present-day Chinese which sound exactly like *pengyou* and *jintian*. If there
is more than one word with the same *pinyin*, the computer will list
the options for you to choose from, in the same way as you do with an
individual character. In fact when you type *pengy* for *pengyou*, 朋友
could well be there as the only candidate. Thus, a 10-stroke or even
30-stroke word can be keyed in with five or six keys. This makes the
typing much faster.

This is, however, not the end of the story. Some software systems will
even allow you to key in the first letter of a two-, three-, or four-character
word and prompt you with the options. For example, you only need key
py, the first letters of *peng* and *you*, and 朋友 will appear as one of
several options. As a result, you can hit three or four keys to type a
20-stroke or even 40-stroke word or phrase.

Component input method

The principle of this component input method is to decompose characters
into a finite number of basic strokes. These basic strokes are represented
by the English letters, hence correspond to the conventional keyboard.
There are several software programs designed on the basis of this principle.
They are all quite complex. In addition, as they are being constantly
revised and updated, we feel that lengthy explanations are beyond the
scope of this book. They are not easy to learn, but can be very fast to use.
The advantage of this method is for those who do not speak but can read
Chinese, or those who are not good at *pinyin*, the romanised system.

Chinese idioms 成语

Chinese proverbs or idioms are known as 成语 *chéngyǔ* which are set
phrases, normally made up of four characters. They are an integral part of
the Chinese language. All Chinese of whatever level of education know
and use 成语 and the more educated they are, the more likely they are to
use them, especially in writing.

Try the next exercise to get a flavour of what 成语 are all about.

✂ Exercise 4

Match each Chinese idiom with its correct translation. Because this is the
last exercise, we've decided to make it quite a challenging one, but you
have actually met almost all the characters.

1 一日千里	(a)	to say one thing and do another
2 九牛一毛	(b)	not to know how to read and write; completely illiterate
3 开门见山	(c)	one's ability falling short of one's wishes
4 力不从心	(d)	at a tremendous pace; by leaps and bounds
5 目不识丁	(e)	a drop in the ocean
6 言行不一	(f)	to put it bluntly; to come (straight) to the point; not to beat about the bush

祝贺你! Congratulations!

You have completed *Teach Yourself Beginner's Chinese Script*. You should
now have mastered the basics of written Chinese and understood how the
script works. We hope you have enjoyed unravelling the mysteries of
Chinese characters.

If you feel you would now like to learn to speak Chinese as well as write
it, why not study *Teach Yourself Beginner's Chinese*? If you feel you
would like to advance on both fronts, then take a look at *Teach Yourself
Chinese*.

祝你走运!

KEY TO THE EXERCISES

Unit 1

1 a) No smoking b) Coffee shop c) No U turn d) No photography e) Petrol/Gas station f) No swimming g) Wheelchair access

2 车: 1E,2B,3D,4A 马: 1A,2C,3E,4B 鱼: 1D,2A,3F,4C 雨: 1C,2E,3B,4D 山: 1B,2F,3C,4E 子: 1F,2D,3A,4F

3 1 月 moon 2 木 wood 3 山 mountain 4 雨 rain 5 日 sun 6 鱼 fish 7 马 horse 8 车 vehicle 9 子 child 10 人 person

Unit 2

2 信 letter, 鲜 fresh, 安 peace, stability

3 从 to follow, 众 crowd, 林 wood (smaller than forest, less wild), 森 forest, 炎 burning hot, 焱 flame

4 1 骡、驴、驹 2 花、草、芽 3 钢、锈、铃 4 逃、过、迈

5 1 打 2 灶 3 讥 4 雪

6 1 泪 tears 2 林 wood, forest 3 笔 pen, brush 4 囚 prisoner 5 灾 disaster

7 墙 wall, 拐 to throw, 怕 fear, 汗 sweat, 吻 kiss, 椅 chair, 暖 warm, 她 she

Unit 3

1 1 人 丿人 2 田 丨冂日田田 3 大 一ナ大 4 木 一十才木 5 钅丿亻生钅钅 6 山 丨山山 7 忄忄忄忄 or 心 丶心心心 8 言 丶亠言言言言言

2

刂	小	材	少	尘	你
丶	心	言	家	米	兴
乙	打	河	冰	牲	跑
丿	办	长	火	户	石
一	大	舌	草	鱼	马

3 1 月 丿刀月月　2 牛 丿广乍牛　3 户 丶亠 户户　4 穴 丶丶宀宀穴
5 当 丨丷丷当当当　6 米 丶丶丷半米米

4 A b C D e F

5 A. Top too big (鱼)　B. 日 on the left should be smaller than 月 on
the right (明)　C. Gap between the two components is too big (休).　D.
Top too small (男) E. Roof much too big. (安)　F. The door should be
open, i.e. there is a space between the dot and 丁 (门)　G. The third
stroke of the water radical should be rising, i.e. 冫 and not 丶 (泪)　H. The
vertical should not extend into the box. (草)

6 b)

7 1 目: eye　2 犭: animal　3 饣: food　4 刂: knife　5 山: mountain

8 1 木 wood/tree　2 言 讠 speech　3 山 mountain　4 氵 water　5 日
day, sky　6 灬 fire　7 贝 money　8 火 fire　9 竹 bamboo　10 刂 knife

9 Radical table stroke order　刂: 丨刂;　刀: 丿刀;　石: 一丆石石石;
饣: 丿𠂉饣;　食: 丿人𠆢今今今仐仺食食;　口: 丨冂口;　目:
丨冂月日目;　贝:丨冂贝贝;　氵:丶丶氵;　水:丨刀才水;　见:丨冂贝见;
牛: 丿广乍牛;　页: 一丆丆页页页;　亻: 丿丿亻;　米:
丶丶丷半米米

10 1 马(horse) on the left-hand side　2 艹 (grass/plant) on the top　3 犭
(animal) on the left　4 讠 (speech) on the left　5 灬 (fire) at the
bottom　6 竹 (bamboo) on the top　7 氵 (water) on the left　8 刂 (knife)
on the right　9 亻 (person) on the left　10 口 (mouth) can be anywhere

11 1 泪 tear　2 林 wood, forest　3 笔 (brush) pen　4 囚 prisoner
5 灾 disaster　6 尘 dust　7 晃 dazzling

12 1 氵water 泪 汗 河　2 讠speech 诗 说 词 订　3 木 wood/tree 杂 林
根 材　4 刂knife 别 刚 刷　5 扌hand 打 推 扣　6 日 sun/day 昨 时 晚

7 饣 food 饭 饺 饿 8 贝 shell 货 贡 贵 9 口 mouth 吸 吃 叮 喝
13 方(4) `一 亠 方 方; 山(3) ｜山 山; 九(2) 乀九 *or* ノ九; 足(7)
丨丨口口早早足足; 去(5) 一 十 土 去 去; 气(4) ノ 仁 仨 气; 尺(4)
⊐ ⊐ 尸 尺; 风(4) ノ 几 凤 风

Unit 4

1 1 小心 to be careful 2 放心 to feel at ease 3 瞎话 lie 4 下海*
to do business (* The analogy is to a fish swimming in the sea, it can
have no idea whether it will succeed in eating other fish and grow bigger
and flourish or whether it will be eaten by bigger fish and destroyed, i.e.
doing business is risky.)
2 1 火车 train 2 木工 carpentry, carpenter 3 月票 monthly pass
4 电视 television 5 电车 trolley bus 6 电影 film 7 电脑 computer
3 1 好吃 delicious 2 难听 unpleasant to listen to 3 好看 good looking 4 难看 ugly
4 1 大学 university 2 花园 garden 3 好心 kind-hearted
5 公平 a) to be fair; justice 明天 c) tomorrow
6 1 吃饭 to eat 2 教书 to teach 3 录音 to record 4 走路 to walk
5 说话 to speak
7 (a) 4 (b) 8 (c) 5 (d) 7 (e) 9 (f) 6 (g) 10 (h) 18 (i) 35 (j)
94 (k) 76 (l) 59
8 (a) 八 (b) 十 (c) 七 (d) 五 (e) 六 (f) 九 (g) 四 (h) 二十一
(i) 三十二 (j) 八十七 (k) 六十五 (l) 九十四
9 (a) 1919 (b) 1991 (c) 1945 (d) 1066 (e) 1789 (f) 1914 (g)
1492 (h) 1848 (i) 2015
10 (a) 一三二一 (b) 一九三二 (c) 一八七六 (d) 一九六五
(e) 一九四九 (f) 一四八六 (g) 一九三七 (h) 一八四二
(i) 二〇三七
11 (a) 1 February (b) 7 March (c) 9 May (d) 10 April (e) 20 June
(f) 30 August (g) 26 November (h) 15 October (i) 31 December
12 (i), (g), (h), (f), (d), (c), (a), (b)
13 a) 一月一日 b) 四月二十三日 c) 七月四日 d) 十二月
二十五日 e) 六月二十一日
14 International Women's Day is on 8 March.
15 4, 6, 5, 1, 3, 7, 2
16 a) 星期四 b) 星期一 c) 星期六

Mini-test

1 1 情 *qíng* feeling (heart radical)   2 清 *qīng* clear (water radical)
3 鲭 *qīng* mackerel (fish radical)   4 请 *qǐng* to ask, request (speech radical)   5 蜻 *qīng* dragonfly (insect radical)   6 晴 *qíng* bright/sunny day (sun/day radical)   7 氰 *qíng* cyanogen (air radical)

2 (5) People's Square (cf. 土 (earth) radical in 场);   (4) People's Park; (1) Great Hall of the People (cf. 大 big; great);   (3) People's Daily (cf. 日 day; daily); (2) Chinese currency

3 生日 b) birthday   早安 c) good morning   日历 b) calendar

4 | 早上 | 上午 | 中午 | 下午 | 晚上 |

5 不公平 means 'not fair, unfair'. The left-hand side is menswear.

6 a) 中学 secondary school, 中国 China, 中心 centre, 中午 noon   b) 火腿 ham, 火山 volcano, 火车 train, 火箭 rocket, 火花 spark

7 a) mouth 口   b) rain 雨   c) fire (2) 火 灬   d) page 页   e) wind 风
f) knife (2) 刀 刂   g) rice 米   h) child 子   i) metal (2) 金 钅   j) eye 目
k) horse 马   l) speech (2) 言 讠   m) big 大   n) field 田   o) heart (2)
心 忄   p) woman 女   q) mountain 山   r) step with left foot 彳   s) door
门   t) to walk 辶

Unit 5

		Radical	*Meaning*
1 a) 匕、又	b) i) 饭	钅	food
	ii) 楼	木	wood/tree
	iii) 楼	米 女	rice, woman
	iv) 员	贝	shell
	v) 迎	丶冫口 叩 迎 迎	

c) (木) 丶冫 肖 肖 弟 弟 (梯)
d) 女; 女; 一/口; 女

2 电梯 lift, elevator,   店员 shop assistant,   服务楼 service block, 电台 radio station

3 A. 广东餐厅   B. 四川餐厅   (ii) Not to smoke

4 1 山田   2 美国 USA   3 英国 UK   4 法国 France   5 No   6 刘

5 A 国安   B 大明   C 英林   D 京生

6 (a) 09.00–17.00   (b) 7am–11pm   (c) 08.30–19.00   (d) 8.00am–12.00 noon, 2.00–6.00pm

7 a) 八   b) 刂   c) 丶   d) 钅   e) 羊

8 a) 三点二十 b) 十点四十五, 十点三刻, 差一刻十一点 c) 九点半 d) 四点五十, 差十分五点 e) 一点一刻 f) 七点三十五

9 The radicals are in brackets: 程(禾), 表(一), 第(⺮), 早(日), 上(一), 中(丨), 午(丿), 下(一), 晚(日), 开(一), 会(人), 参(厶), 观(见), 海(氵), 公(八), 园(囗)

10 1 Shanghai Restaurant 上海餐厅 2 See the film 'Sunrise' 电影《日出》 3 12.00–13.00 十二点--一点 4 1.30pm 一点半 5 Yes. 6 Visiting Beihai (North Sea) Park 参观北海公园 7 A university 大学 (Qinghua University 清华大学)

11 啤酒 (口 氵) (beer) 葡萄酒 (⺾ ⺾ 氵) (wine) (*lit. grape alcohol*) 可口可乐 (口 口 口 木) (Coca-Cola) 咖啡(口 口) (coffee) 茶 (⺾) (tea) 矿泉水 (石 水 水) (mineral water)

12 (a) Bar, beverage, food (b) 咖啡、饮料、啤酒

13 1 French restaurant 2 Men's toilets 3 Women's toilets 4 Lift/elevator 5 Stairs 6 Japanese restaurant 7 Telephone 8 Reception 9 Entrance and exit 10 Bar

Unit 6

Revision

出 2	下 3	华 10	梯 6	北 2	河 9
湖 9	园 5	二 3	上 3	法 9	东 3
南 10	楼 6	香 8	晚 1	弟 4	分 7
半 4	三 3	共 2	海 9	李 6	十 10
星 1	公 7	汽 9	国 5	程 8	中 2

1 日 sun 2 丨 3 一 4 丶 5 口 6 木 7 八 8 禾 9 氵 10 十

1 1 East 2 First go northeast and then north 3 Immediate north 4 Go straight east 5 Southeast corner of the park

2 1 Beijing 2 Shanghai 3 Nanjing 4 Xi'an 5 Hong Kong 6 Taiwan 7 Hainan 8 Donghai (East China Sea) 9 Nanhai (South China Sea)

3 1 中东 Middle East 2 地中海 the Mediterranean 3 南美 South America 4 北海 North Sea

4 Zhongshan Bei Lu 中山北路 (c) Ren He Lu 仁和路 (a) Ping Hai Lu 平海路 (b)

5 i) Southeast   ii) Northwest   iii) 南京 Nanjing (Jiangsu Province)
6 a) s/he wants a drink   iii) 酒吧   b) s/he wants to go to the toilet   iv) 厕所   c) s/he wants to have a meal   ii) 饭馆   d) s/he wants to make a telephone call   i) 电话
7 a) Exit (3)   b) Toilets (5)   c) No Smoking (6)   d) Taxi (4)   e) Duty Free (2)   f) Flower Shop (1)   g) British Education Exhibition (7)
8 (a) No smoking,   (b) No admission,   (c) No parking
9 a) 请勿昭相 (No photography) 昭>照; fire ⺣ radical for 'to shine' or 'to flash'.   b) 小心解电 (Danger: Electric shock) 解>触; 触 means 'to touch'. It consists of a 角 (antenna/horn) and a 虫 (insect), i.e. like the antenna of an insect.   c) 请勿吸咽 (No smoking) 咽>烟; fire 火 radical for 'smoke'.   d) 请勿随地灶痰 (No spitting) 灶>吐; mouth 口 radical for 'spitting'.
10 a) 娄>楼 radical 木 represents wood/tree   b) 艮>银 radical 钅 represents metal,   c) 酉>酒 radical 氵 represents water   d) 反>饭 radical 饣 represents food.
11 a) 火车站   b) 葡萄酒   c) 矿泉水   d) 服务员
12 禁止停车 No parking;   法国银行 Bank of France;   北京大学 Beijing University;   开往上海 Shanghai-bound train
13 1 六   2 京   3 会   4 点   5 半   6 上   7 刻   8 影   9 星   10 观   11 园
14 The correct order is: 3, 4, 1, 5, 2
15 I stayed at the Nanjing Hotel for four days. On the first day, the attendant said: 'Welcome to the Nanjing Hotel'. I stayed on the second floor. The next day I visited Xuanwu Lake Park in the morning, and visited Dr Sun Yatsen's Mausoleum in the afternoon. I watched a film in the evening. On the third and fourth days I attended meetings at Nanjing University. At noon on the third day we had lunch in a Cantonese restaurant. At noon on the fourth day we had lunch in a Shanghainese restaurant. The food in both restaurants was delicious. I had breakfast at 7am on the morning of the fifth day. At 7.45 I took a taxi to the railway station and went back to Beijing on the 8.10 train.

Unit 7

1 a) 6   b) 4   c) 2   d) 8   e) 7   f) 9   g) 5   h) 10   i) 3   j) 1;   (iv) is in full form characters
2 1 A restaurant (the Shandong Restaurant)   2 E   3 G   4 A   5 Kentucky Fried Chicken   6 F

3 a) Konica b) Kentucky Fried Chicken c) Beck's Beer d) Chunlan Freezers e) Cornetto d) is the odd one out (it's a Chinese brand)

4 b)

5 (a); (b) is a better road

6 (a) The International (breakfast) (b) The American (breakfast) (c) The Continental (breakfast) (d) The Chinese (breakfast) (e) Breakfast (f) 式 (g) style, type (h) Fill in your name, number of people, signature, room number and the date

7 (i) You ticked 苹果汁、煎双面蛋、火腿、多士、咖啡 (j) Fresh fruit yoghurt (k) 新鲜水果伴酸奶 (l) 服务费 (m) 11.7¥

8

	很好	好	一般	差
广东餐厅		✓		
四川餐厅	✓			
送餐服务			✓	

9

Flight Confirmation Request 航班确认申请		
Surname 姓 _____	First name 名 _____	Room No. 房号 _____
Airline 航空公司 _____	Departure Date 离开日期 _____	Passport No. 护照号码 _____
Flight No. 航班号 _____	Take-Off time 起飞时间 _____	
Destination 目的地 _____		
Remarks 备注 _____		
Date 日期 _____	Signature 客人签名 _____	Received by 接收人 _____

10 1 (e) 2 (c) 3 (f) 4 (a) 5 (d) 6 (b) GITIC Plaza Hotel is in Guangzhou (Canton)

11 i) No ii) 3, 5, 6 iii) Full form iv) At the beginning v) 3 and 6 vi) 1 and 4 vii) 3 and 6

12 a) 航空 means 'airmail' b) 邮票 means 'postage stamp(s)'
c) 及 means 'and' d) 寄 means 'to post' or 'to mail' e) 收件人、
寄件人

Unit 8

1 a) Red Mansion Cinema b) Big Shanghai c) Letter from the South
d) Letter from the South and Red River Valley
2 a) Upstairs b) even numbers c) 7.45 d) 20 June
3 a) Westbound, 7 stops b) westbound, 2 stops c) westbound, 5
stops d) eastbound, 2 stops
4 1 Beijing University 2 20 yuan 3 Electric appliances 4 English
5 7 days 6 The British Education Exhibition and the English Book
Fair 7 The Japanese Electric Appliances Fair
5 (a) 姓名 Name (b) 中文 Chinese (c) 英文 English (d) 性别
Sex (e) 出生年月 Date of birth 年 year 月 month 日 day (f) 现住
址 Current address (g) 电话 Telephone (h) 工作单位 Place of work
6 a) 8 West Lake Road 西湖路八号 b) The Oriental Hotel 东方饭店
c) The Children's Amusement Park 儿童乐园 d) The People's Park
人民公园

7

饭 丿 勹 乍 饣 饣 饣 饭 饭 (饣)
楼 一 十 十 杧 杧 杧 楼 楼 楼 楼 楼 楼 (木)
河 丶 氵 氵 汀 汀 沪 河 河 (氵)
院 ⺍ 阝 阝 阝 阽 阽 阽 院 (阝)
场 一 十 土 圹 圬 场 场 (土)

8 a) No; it should be 香港 b) 7 June, 9:40am c) Rear door
9 a) 香港 means Hong Kong (cf. Unit 5) b) Yes c) Yes d) 或
e) Fresh fruit f) Black tea, Japanese green tea, Chinese tea and coffee
10 a) Yes, twice b) Two hours before landing c) 服务员
d) Dinner e) 小吃 are snacks (*lit.* small eat/food) f) 三文治 (*sān
wén zhì*) means 'sandwich' g) fruit juice (cf. water radical)

Unit 9

1 一心一意 whole-hearted(ness), with undivided attention; 三心二意
to be in two minds; 一心二用 not giving undivided attention to
something; 一国两制 one country two systems; 三言两语 (of

speech) brief; 七上八下 to be in a state of anxiety and nervousness; 百年大计 a project of vital and far-reaching importance; 千山万水 (covering) a vast area of land; 千家万户 every family and household; 千言万语 (there is) a great deal to express

2 1 During the day   2 a) From the south   b) From the northwest   3 In the evening   4 In the evening 5 28 April

3 1 和平饭店 the Peace Hotel   2 Delicious   3 Beijing   4 The Great Hall of the People   5 Beijing   6 Nanjing   7 To wish her a Happy Valentine's Day   8 Xi'an   9 15 January 1998

4 1 中西快餐、茶座   2 会议厅   3 众. 4 Telephone number for reservations

Main test

1 1 我中午休息   2 我晚上十一点睡觉   3 我下午四点去喝茶
4 我早上七点一刻起床   The correct sequence is 4, 1, 3, 2.

2 中国南京   国际大学东湖路九号   王明山   收

3

Where are you? 你在哪里?		
Date 日期 九月六日		
I will be at 我将在 东方大学		
From am/pm to am/pm		
从 八点半 上午/下午至 四点半 上午/下午		
Comments 要求		
我下午五点回饭店。		
Name 姓名 王海伦/王大卫 Room No. 房号 526		
Signature 签名		

4 我很喜欢上海。天气很好，可是常常有风。我要坐火车去南京。三月五号回北京。我想你。

5 A 1 百香   2 No, it's a café   3 Ground floor (UK), 1st floor (US)
4 It's open 24 hours   B 1 1st floor (UK), 2nd floor (US)   2 11.00am–1.00am   C 1 Cantonese food   2 2nd floor (UK), 3rd floor (US)
3 No   D 1 Italian   2 2nd floor (UK), 3rd floor (US)   3 Dinner

6 1 Boat tickets are being sold   2 freezers   3 Hangzhou, the local tax office

7 Beijing (9), Xi'an (4), Nanjing (12), Shanghai (6)
8 (a) 好吃 (b) 草

Unit 10

1 (a) 2(八) (b) 8(月) (c) 4(扌) (d) 3(土) (e) 9(竹) (f) 9(木)
(g) 4(乚/彐) (h) 12(亻) (i) 6(手) (j) 6(宀) (k) 6(足) (l) 7(氵) (m) 8(亻)
(n) 6(方)
2 (a) (上)午, (下)午 (b) 十点(半) (c) 三点一(刻) (d) (晚)上
(e) (法)国, (中)国 (f) 电(影), 电(话) (g) 啤(酒) (h) 红(茶)
(i) 咖(啡) (j) 餐(厅) (k) (男)厕所 (l) (公)共汽(车), (出)租汽
(车站) (m) 东(北), (北)京 (n) 上(海), (海南)
3 In the last ten years, the fact that the standard of English of Hong
Kong's university students has fallen is something that is known to everyone, students of law are no exception . . . Who would have thought that
after 1997, not only do Hong Kong people still study English but also
even more people within China are doing so? In fact, according to statis-
tics, the number of students learning English in China at this present
moment is even greater than the number of Americans speaking English
in America.
4 1(d), 2(e), 3(f), 4(c), 5(b), 6(a)

TABLE OF RADICALS

You will find slight variations in the radical indexes of different dictionaries. Here is a table of most of the one- or two-stroke radicals which do not necessarily carry any meaning. If they do, this does not normally help your understanding of the meaning of the character of which they are the radical. They are, however, indispensable for looking up characters in a dictionary.

```
、 一 丨 丿 ㇇ 乙 乛 乚 几
厂 匚 卜 冂 厂 乂 勹 凵 厶
```

The number in the right-hand column indicates the unit in which the radical first appears.

二画			Unit
冫 (冰)	bīng	ice	4
一		above	5
讠 (言)	yán	speech	2
二	èr	two	4
十	shí	ten	4
刂 (刀)	dāo	knife	3
亻 (人)	rén	person	2
人 (亻)	rén	person	1
八 (丷)	bā	eight	4
刀 (刂)	dāo	knife	3
力	lì	strength	2

儿	ér	child; son	7
阝 (LHS)		mound	5
阝 (RHS)		town, region	5
又	yòu	again	5
三画			
氵 (水)	shuǐ	water	3
忄 (心)	xīn	heart	2
广	guǎng	covering, roof	4
宀		roof	2
门	mén	door	4
辶		to walk (quickly)	2
工	gōng	work	2
土	tǔ	earth	2
艹	cǎo	grass	2
大	dà	big	2
寸	cùn	inch	5
扌 (手)	shǒu	hand	2
巾	jīn	towel, napkin	8
口	kǒu	mouth	3
囗		enclosure	2
山	shān	mountain	1
彳		step with left foot	3
饣 (食)	shí	food	3
犭	quǎn	(wild) animal, dog	3
女	nǚ	woman	2
子	zǐ	child	1

马	mǎ	horse	1
纟	sī	silk	4
小	xiǎo	small	2
四画			
灬 (火)	huǒ	fire	2
心 (忄)	xīn	heart	2
火 (灬)	huǒ	fire	2
方	fāng	square	5
户	hù	household	2
礻		omen; to express	5
王	wáng	king	4
天	tiān	sky, heaven, day	4
木	mù	wood, tree	1
车	chē	vehicle	1
戈	gē	spear	5
日	rì	sun, day	1
贝	bèi	shell	3
见	jiàn	see	3
父	fù	father	5
气	qì	air	4
牛 (牜)	niú	cattle	3
手 (扌)	shǒu	hand	2
毛	máo	fur, hair	2
攵		to tap; rap	5
斤	jīn	half a kilogram	8
月*	yuè	moon; flesh	4

风	*fēng*	wind	4
水 (氵)	*shuǐ*	water	3
五画			
立	*lì*	to stand	5
疒	*bìng*	illness	5
穴	*xué*	cave	4
衤 (衣)	*yī*	clothing	4
玉	*yù*	jade	5
石	*shí*	stone; mineral	2
目	*mù*	eye	3
田	*tián*	field	2
钅 (金)	*jīn*	metal (gold)	2
禾	*hé*	grain, plant	4
鸟	*niǎo*	bird (long-tailed)	5
六画			
羊	*yáng*	sheep	2
米	*mǐ*	(uncooked) rice	3
衣 (衤)	*yī*	clothing	4
页	*yè*	page	3
虫	*chóng*	insect	4
舌	*shé*	tongue	2
竹 (⺮)	*zhú*	bamboo	2
舟	*zhōu*	boat	5
七画			
言 (讠)	*yán*	speech	2
走	*zǒu*	to go, walk	5

酉	*yǒu*	spirit made from ripe millet; tenth of Twelve Earthly Branches	5
豕	*shǐ*	pig	2
足	*zú*	foot	5
八画			
雨	*yǔ*	rain	1
金 (钅)	*jīn*	gold (metal)	2
鱼	*yú*	fish	1
九画			
食 (饣)	*shí*	food	3

月* Characters with the 'moon' and 'flesh' radical are no longer differentiated and appear under the same radical 月. 'Flesh' as a radical in its own right is written 肉 and is pronounced *ròu*.

PRONUNCIATION GUIDE

Chinese Sounds

Vowels

Here is the list of the Chinese vowels with a rough English equivalent
sound and then one or two examples in Chinese. There are single vowels,
compound vowels or vowels plus a nasal sound which will be listed
separately.

	rough English sound	Chinese examples
a	father	baba, mama
ai	bite	tai, zai
ao	cow	hao, zhao
e	fur	che, he, ge
ei	play	bei, gei, shei, fei
i	tea	didi, feiji, ni
i (after z, c, s, zh, ch, sh and r only)		zi, ci, shi

The 'i' is there more or less for cosmetic reasons – no syllable can exist
without a vowel. Say the consonant and 'sit on it' and you have the sound.

ia	yarrow	jia, xia
iao	meow	biao, piao, yao
ie	yes	bie, xie, ye
iu	yo-yo	liu, jiu, you

y replaces i at the beginning of a word if there is no initial consonant.

o	more	moyimo, mapo
ou	go	dou, zou
u	moo	bu, zhu
ua	suave	gua, hua
uo	war	shuo, cuo, wo

uai	swipe	kuai, wai
ui	weigh	dui, gui, zui

w replaces **u** at the beginning of a word if there is no initial consonant.

ü	pneumonia	ju, qu, lü, nü
üe	pneumatic + **air** (said quickly)	yue, xue, jue

Note that **ü** and **üe** can occur only with the consonants **n, l, j, q** and **x**. As **j, q** and **x** cannot occur as j+u, q+u or x+u, the umlaut (¨) over the 'u' in **ju, qu** and **xu** has been omitted. **N** and **l**, however, can occur as both **nu** and **nü, lu** and **lü** so the umlaut (¨) has been kept.

And **yu** replaces **ü**, and **yue** replaces **üe** if there is no initial consonant.

Here are the **vowels with a nasal sound** formed with vowels followed by **n** or **ng**. Speak through your nose when you pronounce them and listen carefully to the cassette.

	rough English sound	Chinese examples
an	man	fan, man
ang	bang	zhang, shang
en	under	ren, hen
eng	hung	deng, neng
in	bin	nin, jin, xin
ian	yen	tian, nian, qian
iang	**Yang**tse (River)	liang, xiang
ing	finger	ming, qing, xing
iong	**Jung** (the psychoanalyst)	yong, qiong, xiong
ong	Jung	tong, cong, hong
uan	wangle	wan, suan, huan
un	won	wen, lun, chun
uang	wrong	wang, huang, zhuang
üan	pneumatic + **end** (said quickly)	yuan, quan, xuan
ün	'une' in French	yun, jun, qun

Note that **ian** is pronounced as if it were i<u>en</u>.

The same rules about **y** replacing **i** and **w** replacing **u** at the beginning of a word if there is no initial consonant also apply to vowels with a nasal sound.

Yuan replaces **üan** and **yun** replaces **ün** if there is no initial consonant.

Consonants

Here is a list of the Chinese consonants some of which are quite similar to English sounds, others less so. Those that are very different from the nearest English sound are explained.

	rough English sound	Chinese examples
b	bore	bai, bei
p	poor	pao, pang
m	me	ma, mei, ming
f	fan	fan, feng
d	door	da, dou, duo
t	tore	ta, tai, tian
n	need	na, nü, nian
l	lie	lai, lei, liang
z	adds	zi, zai, zuo
c	its	ci, cai, cuo
s	say	si, sui, suan

The next four consonants are all made with the tongue loosely rolled in the middle of the mouth.

zh	jelly	zhao, zhong, zhu
ch	chilly	che, chi, chang
sh	shy	shi, shei, sheng
r	razor	re, ri, rong

The next three consonants are all made with the tongue flat and the corners of the mouth drawn back as far as possible.

j	genius	jia, jiao, jian
q	cheese	qi, qian, qu
	(as said in front of the camera!)	
x	sheet	xiao, xin, xue
	(rather like a whistling kettle)	

Arch the back of the tongue towards the roof of the mouth for the last three consonants.

g	guard	ge, gei, gui
k	card	kai, kan, kuai
h	loch	he, hai, hao

Tones

Chinese is a tonal language. Every syllable in Chinese has its own tone. **Pǔtōnghuà** has four distinct tones plus a neutral tone. This means that syllables which are pronounced the same but have different tones will mean different things. For example, **tang** pronounced in the first tone means *soup* but pronounced in the second tone means *sugar*! But don't worry – all the four tones fall within your natural voice range. You don't have to have a particular type of voice to speak Chinese.

The four tones are represented by the following marks which are put over the vowel such as **nǐ** *you* or over the main vowel of a syllable where there are two or three vowels e.g. **hǎo** *good*, but **guó** *country*:

—   1st tone, high and level

╱   2nd tone, rising

╲╱   3rd tone, falling – rising

╲   4th tone, falling

The diagrams below will help to make this clearer.

Think of **1** as being at the bottom of your voice range and **5** at the top.

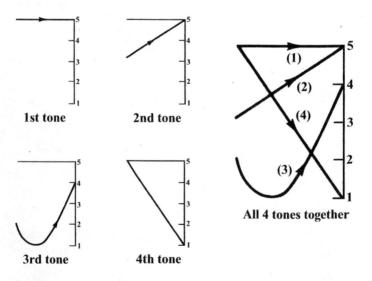

1st tone   **2nd tone**

3rd tone   **4th tone**

All 4 tones together

1st tone: Pitch it where **you** feel comfortable. Say 'oo' as in 'zoo' and keep going for as long as you can. You should be able to keep it up for maybe half a minute. When you have got used to that, change to another vowel sound and practise that in the same way and so on.

2nd tone: Raise your eyebrows every time you attempt a second tone until you get used to it. This is infallible!

3rd tone: Drop your chin onto your neck and raise it again. Then practise the sound doing the movement at the same time.

4th tone: Stamp your foot gently and then accompany this action with the relevant sound.

Neutral tones: Some syllables in Chinese are toneless or occur in the neutral tone. This means they have no tonemark over the vowel. They are rather like unstressed syllables in English, such as *of a* in 'two of a kind'.

Tone changes

Occasionally syllables may change their tones.

(*a*) Two 3rd tones, one after another, are very difficult to say. Where this happens, the first one is said as a 2nd tone:
   Nǐ hǎo! (*How do you do?*) is said as **Ní hǎo.**

(*b*) If three 3rd tones occur together, the first two are normally said as 2nd tones:
   Wǒ yě hǎo. (*I'm OK too.*) is said as **Wó yé hǎo.**

SOME USEFUL PUBLIC SIGNS AND NOTICES

Time

营业时间	Business hours
办公时间	Office hours

Public signs

静	Quiet
推	Push
拉	Pull
开门	Open door (as in lifts/elevators)
关门	Close door (as in lifts/elevators)
欢迎	Welcome
入口	Entrance
出口	Exit
男厕所	Men's toilets/Gentlemen
女厕所	Women's toilets/Ladies
洗手间	Toilet (*lit.* washing hands room)
存车处	Bicycle compound
谢绝参观	Not open to visitors
闲人免进	Admittance to staff only
游客止步	Not open to tourists/Visitors keep out
凭票入内	Admission by ticket only
免费入场	Admission free
小心触电	Danger: Electric shock
禁止停车	No parking
禁止通行	No entry
请勿吸烟	No smoking
请勿照相	No photography
自行车修理部	Bicycle repairs
黄线范围内禁止停放车辆	No parking within the yellow lines

Shopping

商城	Shopping centre, shopping mall
百货商店	Department store
市场	Market
收款台/收银	Cashier
大减价	Big reductions
特价	Special offer(s)
打三折	30% off (by changing the number you change the percentage, for example, 打四折 means 40% off)
八折	20% discount (七折 means 30% discount)

Hotels and restaurants

饭店	Hotel; restaurant
宾馆	Hotel, guest house
酒店	Hotel
旅馆	Small hotel
请勿打扰	Please do not disturb
酒吧	Bar, pub
饭馆	Restaurant
酒家	Restaurant (not in a hotel)
餐厅	Restaurant, dining hall, canteen
肉类	Meat dishes
鱼类	Fish dishes
鸡、鸭类	Chicken and duck dishes
汤类	Soups
蔬菜	Vegetables
饮料	Drinks
冷饮	Cold drinks
热饮	Hot drinks
米饭	Rice
面食	Noodles and dumplings

Entertainment

电影院	Cinema
剧场	Theatre

音乐厅	Concert hall
音乐会	Concert
迪斯科	Disco
售票处	Ticket office
客满	Sold out
楼上	Upstairs
楼下	Downstairs
(27)排	Row (27)
双号	Even numbers
单号	Odd numbers

Services

公安局	Public security bureau
银行	Bank
邮(电)局	Post office
公用电话	Public phone
商务中心	Business centre (normally in a hotel)
问讯处	Information point
出租汽车(站)	Taxi (rank/bay)
火车站	Train station
公共汽车(站)	Bus (station)
地铁(站)	Underground (station)
候车室	Waiting room (at railway and coach stations)
候机室	Lounge (at airport)
机场费	Airport tax
行李检查	Baggage inspection
行李托运处	Baggage check-in

Hospital

医院	Hospital
门诊部	Outpatients department
急诊室	Accident and emergency
挂号处	Registration
药方	Prescription
药房	Pharmacy
服用方法	Dosage/Directions for use

VOCABULARY

Chinese–English

- We have listed the Chinese–English vocabulary under their radicals, using the order adopted in all dictionaries of 1 stroke radicals occurring first, then 2 stroke radicals, then 3 and so on. The order in which, for example, the 1 stroke radicals occur, is also that adopted in most dictionaries.
- We have listed the vocabulary under **words**, (two or more characters), rather than single characters except where they occur as such in the book.
- Words with the same initial character are listed according to the number of strokes in the **second** character, i.e. the smaller the number of strokes in the second character the earlier the word occurs e.g. (东)方 with 4 strokes, occurs before (东)北 with 5 strokes, which in turn occurs before (东)南 with 9 strokes.
- You will see that 东 has a * after it. This is because radical indexes vary slightly between dictionaries and certain characters may appear under different radicals in different dictionaries; e.g. 东 may occur under 一 *horizontal line* in one dictionary but under 木 *tree* in another. We have marked such characters with an asterisk and listed them under both possible radicals. We hope this will help rather than confuse you!
- You should also remember that some radicals such as 口, 目, 木 are not used in modern Chinese for the words for mouth, eye, tree but act as the **radicals** of their modern day equivalents e.g. *mouth* is 嘴 *zuǐ* (not *kǒu*), *eye* is 眼 *yǎn* (not *mù*) and *tree* is 树 *shù* (not *mù*).
- The number in the left hand column indicates the number of strokes of a character excluding its radical. R in the column represents a radical. The number in the right hand column indicates the unit in which the character first appears.

	一画			Unit
R	`			2
4	主	*zhǔ*	to take the initiative	9
	主席	*zhǔxí*	chair(man)	9
R	一	*yī*	one	2
	一般	*yìbān*	usually	7
1	二*	*èr*	two	4
	七	*qī*	seven	4
2	上	*shàng*	up, above	4
	上午	*shàngwǔ*	morning	4
	上班	*shàng bān*	to go to work	6
	上海	*Shànghǎi*	Shanghai	5
	下	*xià*	down, below	4
	下午	*xiàwǔ*	afternoon	4
	下降	*xiàjiàng*	to decline	10
	下海	*xià hǎi*	to do business	4
	万	*wàn*	ten thousand	9
	… 万岁!	*wànsuì*	long live … !	9
	三	*sān*	three	3
	三文治	*sānwénzhì*	sandwich	8
3	元	*yuán*	unit of Chinese currency	8
	不*	*bù*	not, no	4
	不止	*bùzhǐ*	not only	10
	五	*wǔ*	five	4
	开车	*kāi chē*	to drive	4

	开会	*kāi huì*	to hold a meeting	5
	开往	*kāiwǎng*	(of a bus, train) to	6
4	平	*píng*	flat; peace	4
	东*	*dōng*	east	3
	东方	*dōngfāng*	the east; oriental	8
	东北	*dōngběi*	northeast	6
	东南	*dōngnán*	southeast	6
5	至	*zhì*	to	8
6	更(生)	*gēng(shēng)*	to regenerate	9
	更	*gèng*	even	10
	两	*liǎng*	two (of a kind)	5
	来*	*lái*	to come	6
7	画	*huà*	painting; stroke	8; 10
	画展	*huàzhǎn*	art exhibition	8
	事	*shì*	matter	10
	表	*biǎo*	form; table; watch	5
R	丨			2
3	书	*shū*	book	4
	书店	*shūdiàn*	bookshop	7
	书展	*shūzhǎn*	book fair	8
4	半	*bàn*	half	5
	北*	*běi*	north	5
	北京	*Běijīng*	Beijing	5
	申请	*shēnqǐng*	to apply; application	7
	出*口	*chūkǒu*	exit	5
	出生(年月)	*chūshēng (niányuè)*	(year/month of) birth	8

	出租	*chūzū*	for rent; to rent out	6
	出租汽车	*chūzūqìchē*	taxi	6
R	ノ			2
1	九*	*jiǔ*	nine	4
2	及	*jí*	and	7
	川	*chuān*	river; another name for Sichuan Province	8
3	币	*bì*	currency	4
	午餐	*wǔcān*	lunch	9
4	生	*shēng*	birth; raw	4
	生日	*shēngrì*	birthday	4
	生词	*shēngcí*	new word	4
	乐园	*lèyuán*	amusement park	8
5	舌	*shé*	tongue	2
	后*	*hòu*	rear, behind	3
6	我*	*wǒ*	I; me	3
	乱	*luàn*	chaotic, (to be) in disorder	9
11	粤	*yuè*	another name for Guangdong Province	8
R	ㄱ			2
1	了	*le*	modal particle	9
R	刁			2
1	刁	*diāo*	tricky	3
2	习	*xí*	to practise	3

R	乙(乛乚)			2
1	九*	*jiǔ*	nine	4
	二画			
R	冫	*bīng*	ice	4
4	冰柜	*bīngguì*	freezer	9
	冰箱	*bīngxiāng*	refrigerator	6
5	冷	*lěng*	cold	9
8	准	*zhǔn*	to allow	7
	凌晨	*língchén*	early morning	9
R	亠		above	5
2	六	*liù*	six	4
3	市场	*shìchǎng*	market	8
4	产品	*chǎnpǐn*	product	8
6	京	*jīng*	capital; another name for Beijing	5; 8
8	高兴	*gāoxìng*	happy	9
	离开	*líkāi*	to leave	7
9	商	*shāng*	commerce	7
	商店	*shāngdiàn*	shop	7
	商城	*shāngchéng*	shopping centre	8
R	讠(言)	*yán*	speech	2
2	订	*dìng*	to book; subscribe to	2
	讥	*jī*	to scorn	2
	认识	*rènshi*	to know, recognise	9
4	讽	*fěng*	to mock	3
5	词	*cí*	word	3

	词典	*cídiǎn*	dictionary	10
6	话	*huà*	speech	2
	诗	*shī*	poem	3
7	说	*shuō*	to speak	3
	说话	*shuō huà*	to speak	4
8	请	*qǐng*	to invite; please	4
R	二*	*èr*	two	3
1	干	*gàn*	to do	3
1	于	*yú*	at, in	3
R	十	*shí*	ten	4
1	千	*qiān*	thousand	9
4	华	*huá*	China (old word)	4
	华语	*huáyǔ*	Chinese language	4
7	南	*nán*	south	6
	南方	*nánfāng*	the south	8
	南京	*Nánjīng*	Nanjing	6
	南美	*Nánměi*	South America	6
8	真	*zhēn*	real; really	9
R	厂	*chǎng*	factory	2
2	厅	*tīng*	hall	3
6	厕所	*cèsuǒ*	toilet	3
8	原来	*yuánlái*	it turns out to be	10
R	广			
3	在*	*zài*	at, in	6
4	有*	*yǒu*	to have	4
R	匚			

5	医院	*yīyuàn*	hospital	8
R	刂	*dāo*	knife	3
4	刘	*Liú*	a surname	5
	刚	*gāng*	just	3
5	别	*bié*	don't; other	3
6	刻	*kè*	a quarter (of an hour)	5
	刺	*cì*	to prick	3
	到	*dào*	to arrive	6
	到达	*dàodá*	to arrive; arrival	7
	刷	*shuā*	brush	3
	剁	*duò*	to chop	3
8	剧	*jù*	drama	8
10	割	*gē*	to cut	3
R	冖		crown	
3	写	*xiě*	to write	3
R	冂			
4	同	*tóng*	same	8
R	𠂉			
2	午	*wǔ*	noon	4
4	年	*nián*	year	4
	年年	*niánnián*	every year	4
R	亻	*rén*	person	2
2	仍	*réng*	still	10
3	们	*men*	plural for person	2
	他	*tā*	he; him	4

	代代	*dàidài*	every generation	4
4	休	*xiū*	to rest	2
	伦敦	*Lúndūn*	London	9
5	伴	*bàn*	companion	2
	住	*zhù*	to live	6
	你	*nǐ*	you (singular)	6
	低	*dī*	low	9
	位于	*wèiyú*	to be situated at/in	9
6	例外	*lìwài*	exception	10
7	保险室	*bǎoxiǎnshì*	deposit box(es)	5
	信	*xìn*	letter	2
	信用卡	*xìnyòngkǎ*	credit card	7
8	健康	*jiànkāng*	healthy	9
9	停车	*tíng chē*	to stop/park a vehicle	6
R	厂			2
4	后*	*hòu*	rear, behind	3
R	人; 入	*rén; rù*	person; to enter	1; 3
	人人	*rénrén*	everybody	4
	人口	*rénkǒu*	population	4
	入口	*rùkǒu*	entry	4
	人民	*rénmín*	the people (of a country)	4
	人民币	*Rénmínbì*	Renminbi (Chinese currency)	4
	人民日报	*Rénmín Rìbào*	the People's Daily	4
	人民大会堂	*Rénmín Dàhuìtáng*	the Great Hall of the People	4

	人所周知	*rén suǒ zhōu zhī*	it is known to everyone	10
	入场	*rùchǎng*	entrance, admission	8
2	今(日)	*jīn(rì)*	today	8
	以上	*yǐshàng*	over, more than	10
4	会	*huì*	meeting	5
	会	*huì*	will (showing possibility)	9
	会谈	*huìtán*	talk; negotiation	9
	众	*zhòng*	crowd	2
8	拿*	*ná*	to take	10
R	八(丷)	*bā*	eight	4
2	分	*fēn*	minute; the smallest unit of Chinese currency	5
	公	*gōng*	public	4
	公斤	*gōngjīn*	kilogram	8
	公平	*gōngpíng*	fair, just	4
	公司	*gōngsī*	company	7
	公园	*gōngyuán*	park	4
	公里	*gōnglǐ*	kilometre	8
	公共	*gōnggòng*	public	6
	公共汽车	*gōnggòng qìchē*	bus	6
	公道	*gōngdào*	public road; justice	7
	公路	*gōnglù*	public road	8
5	弟弟	*dìdi*	younger brother	5

	谷	*gǔ*	valley	8
6	单	*dān*	single	8
	单号	*dānhào*	odd number	8
7	差*	*chà*	to lack; poor (in quality)	5
	前	*qián*	front	7
R	勺			2
2	勿	*wù*	not, no	6
R	刀 (⺈)	*dāo*	knife	3
5	免费	*miǎnfèi*	free of charge	8
	免税	*miǎn shuì*	duty-free	6
R	力	*lì*	strength	2
2	办公室	*bàngōngshì*	office	5
3	加拿大	*Jiānádà*	Canada	5
R	儿	*ér*	child	7
	儿童	*értóng*	child, children	7
R	卩			
3	印象派	*yìnxiàngpài*	impressionist	8
R	阝 (LHS)		mound	5
4	阴	*yīn*	cloudy	9
5	陈	*Chén*	a surname	5
7	除	*chú*	to get rid of	9
9	随地	*suídì*	at any place	6
R	阝 (RHS)		town, region	5
5	邮票	*yóupiào*	stamp	7
	邮(电)局	*yóu(diàn)jú*	post office	5

6	郑	*Zhèng*	a surname	5
8	郭	*Guō*	a surname	5
	都	*dōu*	all	6
R	又	*yòu*	again	5
2	双	*shuāng*	double	8
	双号	*shuānghào*	even numbers	8
	欢迎	*huānyíng*	welcome	5
8	难	*nán*	difficult	4
	难吃	*nánchī*	awful to eat	4
	难听	*nántīng*	unpleasant to listen to	4
	难看	*nánkàn*	ugly	4
R	厶			2
3	台湾	*Táiwān*	Taiwan	5
	参观	*cānguān*	to visit, visit	5
R	匕	*bǐ*	stagger	
3	北*	*běi*	north	5
	北京	*Běijīng*	Beijing	5
	北海	*Běihǎi*	North Sea	5
	三画			
R	氵	*shuǐ*	water	2
2	汉字	*hànzì*	Chinese character	4
3	江	*jiāng*	river	2
	汗	*hàn*	sweat	2
	污	*wū*	dirty	9
4	沪	*hù*	another name for Shanghai	8

	汽车	qìchē	vehicle	6
5	法(律)	fǎ(lǜ)	law	5, 10
	法国	Fǎguó	France	5
	河	hé	river	3
	河南	Hénán	Henan Province	6
	河北	Héběi	Hebei Province	6
	泪	lèi	tear	2
6	洋	yáng	ocean	7
	津	jīn	another name for Tianjin	8
7	酒	jiǔ	alcohol	
	酒吧	jiǔbā	bar, pub	5
	酒店	jiǔdiàn	hotel	7
	海	hǎi	sea	3
	海南	Hǎinán	Hainan Province	6
8	清	qīng	clear; Qing Dynasty	4; 9
9	湖	hú	lake	6
	湖北	Húběi	Hubei Province	6
	湖南	Húnán	Hunan Province	6
	港	gǎng	harbour; another name for Hong Kong	8
	湘	Xiāng	another name for Hunan Province	8
12	潮	cháo	tide	7
R	忄	xīn	heart	2
3	忙	máng	busy	9

4	快乐	kuàilè	happy	9
5	怕	pà	to fear	2
	性别	xìngbié	sex, gender	8
6	恨	hèn	to hate	2
8	情	qíng	feeling	4
R	广	guǎng	broad	3, 5
	广东	Guǎngdōng	Guangdong Province	5
	广西	Guǎngxī	Guangxi Autonomous Region	6
	广场	guǎngchǎng	square	4
5	店	diàn	shop	7
	店员	diànyuán	shop assistant	5
7	座	zuò	seat	7
	席	xí	mat, seat	9
R	宀		roof	2
3	安	ān	peace	2
	字	zì	Chinese character	4
4	灾	zāi	disaster	2
5	宝玉	bǎoyù	precious jade	8
6	客(人)	kè(rén)	guest	7
	客满	kèmǎn	sold out	8
	室	shì	room	7
7	家	jiā	home, family	2
8	寄	jì	to post/mail a letter, etc.	7
	寄件人	jìjiànrén	sender	7

R	门	*mén*	door	4
4	间	*jiān*	during	10
R	辶		to walk (quickly)	2
3	迈	*mài*	to step over	2
	过	*guò*	to pass	2
4	还	*hái*	still	10
	远	*yuǎn*	far	2
	近	*jìn*	close, near	10
	这儿, 这里	*zhèr, zhèli*	here	4, 9
6	逃	*táo*	to escape	2
	送餐	*sòng cān*	food delivery	7
R	工	*gōng*	work	2
	工人	*gōngrén*	worker	4
	工作	*gōngzuò*	work, to work	9
	工作单位	*gōngzuò dānwèi*	work unit	8
R	土	*tǔ*	earth	2
2	去	*qù*	to go	6
3	在*	*zài*	at, in	6
	尘*	*chén*	dust	3
	场	*chǎng*	square; open space	8
	地址	*dìzhǐ*	address	7
	地点	*dìdiǎn*	venue	8
	地中海	*Dìzhōnghǎi*	the Mediterranean	6
4	坐	*zuò*	to sit	2
6	城(市)	*chéng(shì)*	town, city	9, (7)

9	喜*欢	xǐhuān	to like	6
11	墙	qiáng	wall	2
R	艹	cǎo	grass	
4	花	huā	flower	2
	芽	yá	sprout	2
	花园	huāyuán	garden	4
5	英	yīng	hero	5
	英文	Yīngwén	English language	8
	英里	yīnglǐ	mile	8
	英国	Yīngguó	Britain, England	5
	英语	Yīngyǔ	English language	10
6	草	cǎo	grass	2
	茶	chá	tea	5
7	莫	mò	do not	9
8	菜	cài	vegetable; dish	8
	营业	yíngyè	business	9
	黄	huáng	yellow	7
9	葡萄酒	pútáojiǔ	wine	5
14	藏	Zàng	Zang nationality; Tibetan	6
R	大	dà	big	2
	大人	dàrén	adult	4
	大学	dàxué	university	4
1	太平洋	Tàipíngyáng	the Pacific Ocean	7
R	寸	cùn	unit of length (=1/30 metre)	5

R	扌	*shǒu*	hand	2
2	打	*dǎ*	to hit	2
	扔	*rēng*	to throw	2
3	扣	*kòu*	(to) button	3
	扬子江	*Yángzijiāng*	the Yangtze River	7
4	找	*zhǎo*	to look for	3
	报	*bào*	newspaper	9
	护照	*hùzhào*	passport	7
5	拥	*yōng*	to possess	9
	拌	*bàn*	to blend	2
8	推	*tuī*	to push	3
	排	*pái*	row	7
	接收人	*jiēshōurén*	recipient (of a letter)	7
R	弋			
2	式	*shì*	style, form	7
R	巾	*jīn*	towel, napkin	5
R	口	*kǒu*	mouth	2
	口香糖	*kǒuxiāngtáng*	chewing gum	9
2	只	*zhǐ*	only	7
	叮	*dīng*	to sting	3
	号	*hào*	number; date	7; 9
	号码	*hàomǎ*	number	7
	可是	*kěshì*	but	9
	可口可乐	*kěkǒukělè*	Coca-Cola	5
3	吃	*chī*	to eat	3
	吃饭	*chī fàn*	to eat	4

	吸	xī	to breathe in	3
	吸烟	xī yān	to smoke	6
	吐痰	tù tán	to spit	6
4	吴	Wú	a surname	5
	吻	wěn	kiss, to kiss	2
	员	yuán	person (in a trade)	5
	听	tīng	to listen	4
	听见	tīngjiàn	to hear	4
	听说	tīngshuō	to hear someone say	4
	听懂	tīngdǒng	to understand	4
	君	jūn	gentleman (classical Chinese)	9
5	咖啡	kāfēi	coffee	5
	咖啡馆	kāfēiguǎn	café	6
6	品	pǐn	product	7
	哪知道 … ?	nǎ zhīdao..?	who would have thought . . . ?	10
7	哥哥	gēge	elder brother	5
8	唯一	wéiyī	only	7
9	喝	hē	to drink	3
	喜*欢	xǐhuan	to like	6
	啤酒	píjiǔ	beer	5
13	器	qì	appliance	7
R	口		enclosure	2
2	囚	qiú	prisoner	2
	四	sì	four	4

	四川	*Sìchuān*	Sichuan Province	5
3	回	*huí*	to return	6
4	园	*yuán*	garden	2
5	国	*guó*	country, state	3
	国内	*guónèi*	(of a country) domestic	10
	国际	*guójì*	international	7
	国语	*guóyǔ*	national language	4
	图书展销会	*túshū zhǎnxiāohuì*	book fair	8
7	圆	*yuán*	unit of Chinese currency	8
R	山	*shān*	mountain	1
	山东	*Shāndōng*	Shandong Province	6
	山西	*Shānxī*	Shanxi Province	6
4	岗	*gǎng*	hillock	3
5	岭	*lǐng*	hill	3
7	峰	*fēng*	peak	3
8	崖	*yá*	cliff	3
R	彳		step with left foot	3
3	行李	*xínglǐ*	luggage	7
6	很	*hěn*	very	6
9	街	*jiē*	street	8
12	德	*dé*	virtue	5
	德国	*Déguó*	Germany	5
R	夕			
3	名	*míng*	(given) name	7

	多	*duō*	many, much	9
R	夂			
2	处	*chù*	place	7
5	备注	*bèizhù*	remark	7
R	尸	*shī*	corpse	
4	局	*jú*	bureau	7
7	展览馆	*zhǎnlǎnguǎn*	exhibition hall	8
	展销会	*zhǎnxiāohuì*	trade fair	8
R	饣	*shí*	food	3
4	饭	*fàn*	food	3
	饭店	*fàndiàn*	restaurant; hotel	5
	饭馆	*fànguǎn*	restaurant	6
	饮料	*yǐnliào*	drinks	5
5	饱	*bǎo*	to be full up	3
6	饼	*bǐng*	pancake	3
	饺	*jiǎo*	dumpling	3
7	饿	*è*	hungry	3
8	馅	*xiàn*	stuffing	3
R	犭	*quǎn*	(wild) animal	3
5	狗	*gǒu*	dog	3
	狐	*hú*	fox	3
6	独立	*dúlì*	independent	9
7	狼	*láng*	wolf	3
8	猫	*māo*	cat	3
R	彐			
5	录音	*lù yīn*	to record	4

R	弓	*gōng*	bow	
4	张	*Zhāng*	a surname	5
R	己; 已	*jǐ; yǐ*	self; already	3
	已经	*yǐjīng*	already	9
R	女	*nǚ*	female	2
	女厕所	*nǚ cèsuǒ*	women's toilets	5
2	奴	*nú*	slave	6
3	她	*tā*	she; her	2
	奸	*jiān*	to rape	6
	好	*hǎo*	good	2
	好吃	*hǎochī*	delicious	4
	好心	*hǎoxīn*	kind-hearted	4
	好听	*hǎotīng*	pleasant to listen to	4
	好看	*hǎokàn*	good-looking	4
	妈妈	*māma*	mum, mother	5
	如意	*rúyì*	as one wishes	9
5	姓	*xìng*	surname	7
	姓名	*xìngmíng*	name	7
	妹妹	*mèimei*	younger sister	5
	姐姐	*jiějie*	elder sister	5
8	娶	*qǔ*	to marry (of a man)	6
10	嫁	*jià*	to marry (of a woman)	6
R	子	*zǐ*	child	1
5	学(习)	*xué(xí)*	to learn, to study; study	3; (4)

	学院	*xuéyuàn*	college, institute	8
R	马	*mǎ*	horse	1
4	驴	*lǘ*	donkey	2
5	驹	*jū*	pony	2
8	骑	*qí*	to ride	2
11	骡	*luó*	mule	2
R	纟	*sī*	silk	4
3	级	*jí*	grade	9
	红	*hóng*	red	8
5	线	*xiàn*	line, thread	8
6	统计	*tǒngjì*	statistics	10
8	绿	*lǜ*	green	8
R	小 (⺌)	*xiǎo*	small	2
	小人	*xiǎo rén*	small-minded person	4
	小心	*xiǎo xīn*	careful	4
	小吃	*xiǎochī*	snack	8
	小时	*xiǎoshí*	hour	7
	小学	*xiǎoxué*	primary school	4
3	尖	*jiān*	sharp	2
	尘*	*chén*	dust	3
	当	*dāng*	to act/serve as	3
	光临	*guānglín*	to be present	8
8	常常	*chángcháng*	often	9
	四画			
R	灬	*huǒ*	fire	2

5	点	*diǎn*	o'clock	5
6	热	*rè*	hot	9
8	煮	*zhǔ*	to boil	3
9	照相	*zhào xiàng*	to take a photo	6
R	心	*xīn*	heart	2
4	念书	*niàn shū*	to study	4
9	想	*xiǎng*	to think; to miss somebody	2
	意*大利	*Yìdàlì*	Italy	5
R	火	*huǒ*	fire	2
	火山	*huǒshān*	volcano	4
	火车	*huǒchē*	train	4
	火花	*huǒhuā*	spark	4
	火腿	*huǒtuǐ*	ham	4
	火箭	*huǒjiàn*	rocket	4
3	灶	*zào*	stove	2
4	炎	*yán*	burning hot	2
6	烧	*shāo*	to burn	3
8	焱	*yàn*	flame	2
R	文	*wén*	writing, literature	9
	文物	*wénwù*	cultural object(s)	9
2	刘	*Liú*	a surname	5
R	方	*fāng*	square	5
4	放心	*fàng xīn*	to be at ease	4
6	旅	*lǚ*	to travel	10
	旅行(社)	*lǚxíng(shè)*	travel (agency)	7

	旅游	*lǚyóu*	to travel, travel	7
R	户	*hù*	household	2
4	房	*fáng*	house	2
	房号	*fáng hào*	room number	7
	房间	*fángjiān*	room	7
R	礻		omen; to express	5
5	祝	*zhù*	to wish	9
	祝贺	*zhùhè*	to congratulate	10
R	王	*Wáng*	a surname; king	4
	王子	*wángzi*	prince	4
4	现在	*xiànzài*	now, present	9
	现住址	*xiànzhùzhǐ*	present address	8
5	珍惜	*zhēnxī*	to treasure	9
R	天	*tiān*	day, heaven	4
	天子	*tiānzi*	emperor (son of heaven)	4
	天天	*tiāntiān*	every day	4
	天气	*tiānqì*	weather	4
	天气预报	*tiānqìyùbào*	weather forecast	9
	天地	*tiāndì*	heaven and earth	8
	天津	*Tiānjīn*	Tianjin	8
R	木	*mù*	wood	1
	木工	*mùgōng*	carpenter	4
2	东*	*dōng*	east	3
	杂	*zá*	mixed	3
	乐园	*lèyuán*	paradise	8

3	李	*Lǐ*	a surname	5
	村	*cūn*	village	2
	材	*cái*	timber	3
4	林	*lín*	wood; a surname	2
	枫	*fēng*	maple	2
6	根	*gēn*	root	3
	根据	*gēnjù*	according to	10
7	检字表	*jiǎnzìbiǎo*	character index	10
8	森(林)	*sēn(lín)*	forest	2, (5)
	椅	*yǐ*	chair	2
9	楼	*lóu*	building, house	5
	楼上	*lóushàng*	upstairs	6
	楼下	*lóuxià*	downstairs	8
	楼梯	*lóutī*	stairs	5
R	不*	*bù*	not, no	4
	不止	*bùzhǐ*	not only	10
3	否	*fǒu*	not; no; deny; or not	6
5	歪	*wāi*	crooked	6
	甭	*béng*	don't	6
6	孬	*nāo*	bad	6
R	车	*chē*	vehicle	1
	车次	*chēcì*	train number	9
	车道	*chēdào*	vehicle lane	7
R	戈	*gē*	spear	
3	我*	*wǒ*	I; me	6

R	止	*zhǐ*	to stop, to end	
1	正宗	*zhèngzōng*	(of food) authentic	9
2	此刻	*cǐkè*	at this moment	10
R	日	*rì*	sun, day	1
	日历	*rìlì*	calendar	4
	日出	*rìchū*	sunrise	5
	日本	*Rìběn*	Japan	5
	日航	*Rìháng*	Japan Airlines	7
	日期	*rìqī*	date	7
	日程表	*rìchéngbiǎo*	itinerary, programme	5
2	早	*zǎo*	early	4
	早上	*zǎoshang*	early morning	4
	早安!	*zǎo'ān*	Good morning!	4
	早饭	*zǎofàn*	breakfast	6
	早晨	*zǎochén*	early morning	9
	早餐	*zǎocān*	breakfast	7
3	时(间)	*shí(jiān)*	time	3, (7)
4	明	*míng*	bright	2
	明天	*míngtiān*	tomorrow	4
5	昨(天)	*zuó(tiān)*	yesterday	3, (9)
	星(星)	*xīng(xīng)*	star	4, (8)
	星期	*xīngqī*	week	4
6	晃	*huǎng*	to dazzle	3
7	晚	*wǎn*	evening; late	3
	晚上	*wǎnshang*	evening	4
	晚餐	*wǎncān*	dinner	9

8	晴	*qíng*	bright, sunny	4
	普通话	*Pǔtōnghuà*	Modern Standard Chinese	4
9	暖	*nuǎn*	warm	2
R	曰	*yuē*	to say (classical Chinese)	
1	电*	*diàn*	electricity, electric	4
	电车	*diànchē*	tram	4
	电台	*diàntái*	radio station	5
	电话	*diànhuà*	telephone	4
	电脑	*diànnǎo*	computer	4
	电视	*diànshì*	television	4
	电梯	*diàntī*	lift, elevator	5
	电影	*diànyǐng*	film	4
	电影院	*diànyǐngyuàn*	cinema	7
	电器	*diànqì*	electric appliance(s)	7
8	最	*zuì*	the most	9
R	中*	*zhōng*	middle, centre	5
	中心	*zhōngxīn*	centre; heart	4
	中午	*zhōngwǔ*	noon	4
	中东	*Zhōngdōng*	the Middle East	6
	中学	*zhōngxué*	secondary/high school	4
	中国	*Zhōngguó*	China	4
R	贝	*bèi*	shell	3
3	贡	*gòng*	tribute	3
4	货	*huò*	goods	3

5	贵	guì	expensive	3
	费	fèi	fee(s)	7
	贴	tiē	to stick on	7
	贺	hè	to congratulate	10
6	资	zī	capital; money	3
R	见	jiàn	to see	3
R	父	fù	father	5
4	爸爸	bàba	dad, father	5
R	气	qì	air	4
	气温	qìwēn	(weather) temperature	9
6	氧	yǎng	oxygen	10
8	氰	qíng	cyanogen	4
R	牛	niú	cattle, cow	3
4	物	wù	object, thing	10
R	手	shǒu	hand	2
6	拿*	ná	to take	10
R	毛	máo	fur, hair	2
R	攵		to tap, rap	5
2	收	shōu	to receive	7
	收件人	shōujiànrén	recipient (of a letter, etc.)	7
7	教书	jiāo shū	to teach	4
	教育(展)	jiàoyù(zhǎn)	education (exhibition)	8
8	数字	shùzi	number	10
R	斤	jīn	half a kilogram	8

9	新	*xīn*	new	7
R	爪(爫)	*zhǎo, zhuǎ*	claws	
6	爱(愛)	*ài*	to love, love	2
R	尺	*chǐ*	1/3 of a metre	8
R	月	*yuè*	moon; flesh	1
	月月	*yuèyuè*	every month	4
	月票	*yuèpiào*	monthly (travel) pass	4
4	朋友	*péngyǒu*	friend	9
	服务	*fúwù*	service, to serve	5
	服务台	*fúwùtái*	reception	5
	服务员	*fúwùyuán*	attendant	5
	服务楼	*fúwùlóu*	service block	5
R	风	*fēng*	wind	4
	风力	*fēnglì*	wind-force	9
	风水	*fēngshuǐ*	fengshui	4
	风向	*fēngxiàng*	wind direction	9
	风味	*fēngwèi*	style of cooking	5
R	比	*bǐ*	to compare	10
R	水	*shuǐ*	water	4
	水准	*shuǐzhǔn*	level, standard	10
	五画			
R	立	*lì*	to stand	5
5	站	*zhàn*	station; stop (bus etc.)	6
	站台	*zhàntái*	platform	9

R	病(疒)	*bìng*	illness	5
R	衤(衣)	*yī*	clothes	4
R	穴	*xué*	cave	4
R	玉	*yù*	jade	5
R	示	*shì*	to show	
8	禁止	*jìnzhǐ*	to prohibit	6
R	石	*shí*	stone, mineral	2
3	矿泉水	*kuàngquánshuǐ*	mineral water	5
	码	*mǎ*	number	8
7	确认	*quèrèn*	to confirm	7
8	碗	*wǎn*	bowl	2
10	磅	*bàng*	pound (weight)	8
R	戍	*shù*	to defend	
1	成功	*chénggōng*	success; successful	9
	成语	*chéngyǔ*	idiom, proverb	10
R	尚			
6	常*常	*chángcháng*	often	9
R	目	*mù*	eye	2
	目的地	*mùdìdì*	destination	7
2	盯	*dīng*	to stare	3
3	眨	*zhǎ*	to blink	3
4	看	*kàn*	to look at; to watch	4
	看见	*kànjiàn*	to see	4
	看懂	*kàndǒng*	to understand	4
6	眼	*yǎn*	eye	3

10	瞎	*xiā*	blind	3
	瞎话	*xiāhuà*	lie	4
R	田	*tián*	field	2
2	男	*nán*	male	2
	男厕所	*náncèsuǒ*	men's toilets	5
R	罒			
3	罗马	*Luómǎ*	Rome	9
R	钅	*jīn*	metal	2
2	钉	*dīng*	nail, to nail	2
4	钢	*gāng*	steel	2
	钟	*zhōng*	clock	5
5	铃	*líng*	bell	2
	钱	*qián*	money	4
6	银行	*yínháng*	bank	5
7	锈	*xiù*	rust; to rust	2
R	矢	*shǐ*	arrow	
3	知道	*zhīdào*	to know (a fact)	10
R	禾	*hé*	plant; grain	4
3	和平	*hépíng*	peace	9
4	香港	*Xiānggǎng*	Hong Kong	5
R	白	*bái*	white	
1	百	*bǎi*	hundred	9
3	的	*de*	*particle*	6
R	鸟	*niǎo*	bird (long-tailed)	5
2	鸡	*jī*	chicken	

R	癶			
	登机门	dēng jīmén	boarding gate	8
	六画			
R	羊	yáng	sheep	2
3	差*	chà	to lack; poor (in quality)	5
	美	měi	beautiful	5
	美术(馆)	měishù(guǎn)	art (gallery)	8
	美国	Měiguó	America	5
R	米	mǐ	rice (uncooked); metre	3; 8
	米饭	mǐfàn	cooked rice	6
R	衣(衤)	yī	clothes	4
R	西	xī	west	6
	西北	xīběi	northwest	6
	西汉	Xīhàn	West Han (Dynasty)	9
	西安	Xī'ān	Xi'an	6
	西南	xīnán	southwest	6
	西晋	Xījìn	West Jin (Dynasty)	9
	西藏	Xīzàng	Tibet	6
3	要	yào	to want	8
5	票(价)	piào(jià)	ticket (price)	8
R	页	yè	page	3
R	虫	chóng	insect	4
8	蜻	qīng	dragonfly	4
R	舌	shé	tongue	2

R	竹(⺮)	zhú	bamboo	2
4	笔	bǐ	(brush) pen	2
5	第	dì	(for ordinal number)	4
7	签名	qiānmíng	to sign; signature	7
R	自	zì	self	9
	自主	zìzhǔ	self determination	9
R	舟	zhōu	boat	
4	航空	hángkōng	by air	7
	航班	hángbān	flight	7
	七画			
R	言(讠)	yán	speech	2
R	走	zǒu	to go, walk	4
	走路	zǒu lù	to walk	4
2	赵	Zhào	a surname	5
3	起飞	qǐfēi	to take off	7
R	酉	yǒu	spirit made from ripe millet; 10th of Twelve Earthly Branches	5
R	豕	shǐ	pig	2
R	足	zú	foot	5
6	路	lù	road, street	4
R	身	shēn	body	
	身体	shēntǐ	body; health	9
R	角	jiǎo	horn; unit of Chinese currency, 1/10 of one yuan	8
6	触电	chùdiàn	electric shock	6

	八画以上			
R	青	qīng	green; another name for Qinghai Province	8
	青海	Qīnghǎi	Qinghai Province	8
R	雨	yǔ	rain	1
3	雪	xuě	snow	2
5	零	líng	zero	4
R	鱼	yú	fish	1
4	鲁	Lǔ	another name for Shangdong Province	8
6	鲜	xiān	fresh	2
8	鲭	qīng	mackerel	4
R	音	yīn	sound	4
4	意*大利	Yìdàlì	Italy	5
R	食	shí	food	
	食品	shípǐn	food (product)	7
7	餐厅	cāntīng	dining hall, restaurant	5
	Other			
	卡片	kǎpiàn	card	4
	巴士	bāshi	bus (pidgin English)	6

English–Chinese

address	地址	7
admission, entrance	入内	8
adult	大人	4
afternoon	下午	4
air	气	4
alcohol	酒	5
to allow	准	7
America	美国	5
to apply; application	申请	7
to arrive	到	6
to arrive; arrival	到达	7
at, in	在	6
attendant	服务员	5
awful (to eat)	难吃	4
bank	银行	5
bar, pub	酒吧	5
beautiful	美	5
beer	啤酒	5
Beijing	北京	5
big	大	2
bird	鸟	5
birthday	生日	4
body; health	身体	9
to boil	煮	3
Bon voyage!	一路平安!	9
book	书	4
to book; subscribe to	订	2
book fair	图书展销会	8
bookshop	书店	7
bowl	碗	2
breakfast	早饭, 早餐	6, 7
to breathe in	吸	3
Britain, England	英国	5
building, house	楼	5
to burn	烧	3
bus	公共汽车	6

business	营业	9
busy	忙	9
but	可是	9
by air	航空	7

café	咖啡馆	6
calendar	日历	4
Canada	加拿大	5
card	卡(片)	4
careful	小心	4
cat	猫	3
cattle, cow	牛	3
centre	中心	4
chicken	鸡	8
child, children	儿童	7
China	中国	4
Chinese (Modern Standard)	普通话	4
Chinese character	字, 汉字	3
cinema	电影院	7
clock	钟	5
close, near	近	10
clothes	衣(服)	4
cloudy	阴	9
Coca-Cola	可口可乐	5
cold	冷	9
college, institute	学院	8
to come	来	6
commerce	商	7
company	公司	7
to compare	比	10
computer	电脑	4
to congratulate	祝贺	10
cooked rice	米饭	6
country, state	国	3
credit card	信用卡	7

dad, father	爸爸	5
date	日期	7
day, heaven	天	4

delicious	好吃	2
dictionary	词典	10
difficult	难	4
dining hall, restaurant	餐厅	5
dinner, supper	晚餐	9
dog	狗	3
door	门	4
double	双	8
down, below	下	4
downstairs	楼下	8
to drink	喝	3
drinks	饮料	5
to drive	开车	4
duty-free	免税	6
early	早	4
east	东	3
to eat	吃(饭)	4
education (exhibition)	教育(展)	8
eight	八	4
elder brother	哥哥	5
elder sister	姐姐	5
electric appliance(s)	电器	7
electricity, electric	电	4
English language	英文, 英语	8, 10
entry, entrance	入口	4
even numbers	双号	8
evening	晚上	4
evening; late	晚	3
exhibition hall	展览馆	8
exit	出口	5
expensive	贵	3
eye	眼	3
fair, just	公平	4
far	远	2
father	爸爸	5
to fear	怕	2
fee(s)	费	7

female	女	2
fengshui	风水	4
field	田	2
film	电影	4
fire	火	2
fish	鱼	1
five	五	4
flower	花	2
food (product)	食品	7
four	四	4
France	法国	5
free of charge	免费	8
freezer	冰柜	9
friend	朋友	9
fur, hair	毛	2
garden	花园	4
gender, sex	性别	8
Germany	德国	5
to go	去	6
to go to work	上班	6
good	好	2
good-looking	好看	4
Good luck!	祝你走运!	9
Good morning!	早安!	4
green	绿	8
guest	客	7
half	半	5
half a kilogram	斤	8
ham	火腿	4
hand	手	2
happy	高兴, 快乐	9
Happy birthday!	生日快乐!	9
Happy (Chinese) New Year!	春节快乐!	9
Happy Christmas!	圣诞节快乐!	9
Happy Easter!	复活节快乐!	9
Happy New Year!	新年快乐!	9
Happy Valentine's Day!	情人节快乐!	9

to hate	恨	2
to have	有	4
he; him	他	4
health	身体	9
healthy	健康	9
to hear	听见	4
heart	心	2
to hit	打	2
to hold a meeting	开会	5
home, family	家	2
Hong Kong	香港	5
horse	马	1
hospital	医院	8
hot	热	9
hotel, restaurant	饭店, 酒店	4, 7
hour	小时	7
hundred	百	9
hungry	饿	3
I; me	我	6
idiom, proverb	成语	10
illness	病	5
international	国际	7
to invite; please	请	4
Italy	意大利	5
itinerary, programme	日程表	5
Japan	日本	5
jiao (unit of Chinese currency, 1/10 of one yuan)	角	8
kilogram	公斤	8
kilometre	公里	8
kiss, to kiss	吻	2
knife	刀	3
to know (a fact)	知道	10
to know, recognise	认识	9
to lack; poor (in quality)	差	5
lake	湖	6

law	法(律)	5, 10
to leave	离开	7
letter	信	2
level, standard	水准	10
lie	瞎话	4
lift, elevator	电梯	5
to like	喜欢	6
to listen	听	4
London	伦敦	8
long live . . . !	…万岁!	9
to look at; to watch	看	4
to look for	找	3
love, to love	爱(愛)	2
luggage/baggage	行李	7
lunch	午餐	9
to mail (a letter, etc.)	寄	7
male	男	2
many, much	多	9
market	市场	8
the Mediterranean	地中海	6
men's toilets	男厕所	5
middle, centre	中	5
the Middle East	中东	6
mile	英里	8
mineral water	矿泉水	5
minute; the smallest unit of Chinese currency	分	5
money	钱	4
moon	月	1
morning	上午	4
the most	最	9
mother	妈妈	5
mountain	山	1
mum, mother	妈妈	5
name	姓名	7
Nanjing	南京	6
near	近	10

new	新	7
new word	生词	4
newspaper	报	9
nine	九	4
noon	中午	4
north	北	5
northeast	东北	6
northwest	西北	6
not, no	不	4
now, present	现在	9
number (room, telephone, etc.)	号; 号码	7
number	数字	10
object, thing	物	10
o'clock	点	5
odd number	单号	8
office	办公室	5
often	常常	9
one	一	2
oriental; the east	东方	8
the Pacific Ocean	太平洋	7
page	页	3
painting	画	8
park	公园	4
to pass	过	2
passport	护照	7
peace	和平	9
pen (brush)	笔	2
the people	人民	4
person	人	1
platform	站台	9
pleasant to listen to	好听	4
population	人口	4
to post, mail	寄	7
post office	邮(电)局	5
primary school	小学	4
product	产品	8
to prohibit	禁止	6

pub	酒吧	5
public	公共	6
public road	公路	8
to push	推	3
quarter (of an hour)	刻	5
radio station	电台	5
rain	雨	1
to read books, to study	念书	4
real; really	真	9
rear, behind	后	3
reception	服务台	5
to record	录音	4
red	红	8
refrigerator	冰箱	6
Renminbi (Chinese currency)	人民币	4
to rent out; for rent	出租	6
restaurant	饭馆	6
restaurant, hotel	饭店	5
to return	回	9
to ride	骑	2
river	河	3
road, street	路	4
room	房间	7
room number	房号	7
row	排	7
sea	海	3
secondary/high school	中学	4
to see	看见	4
to send a letter, etc.	寄	7
service, to serve	服务	5
seven	七	4
sex, gender	性别	8
Shanghai	上海	5
she; her	她	2
sheep	羊	2
shop	商店	7

shopping centre	商城	8
to sign; signature	签名	7
to sit	坐	2
six	六	4
slave	奴	6
small	小	2
to smoke	吸烟	6
snack	小吃	8
snow	雪	2
sold out	客满	8
south	南	6
South America	南美	6
southeast	东南	6
southwest	西南	6
to speak	说(话)	4
stairs	楼梯	5
stamp (postage)	邮票	7
statistics	统计	10
to stick on	贴	7
to stop/park a vehicle	停车	6
street	街	8
stroke	画	8
study, to study	学习	4
style of cooking	风味	5
success(ful)	成功	9
sunny, bright	晴	4
sunrise	日出	5
surname	姓	7
to take	拿	10
to take a photo	照相	6
talks; negotiations	会谈	9
taxi	出租汽车	6
tea	茶	5
to teach	教书	4
tear	泪	2
telephone	电话	4
television	电视	4
temperature (weather)	气温	9

ten	十	4
ten thousand	万	9
to think; to miss somebody	想	2
thousand	千	9
three	三	4
Tianjin	天津	8
Tibet	西藏	6
ticket price	票价	8
time	时(间)	3, (7)
to (of a bus, train)	开往	6
toilet	厕所	3
tomorrow	明天	4
town, city	城(市)	9, (7)
trade fair	展销会	8
train	火车	4
train number	车次	9
tram	电车	4
travel (agency)	旅行(社)	7
travel, to travel	旅游	7
two	二	4
two (of a kind)	两	5
ugly	难看	4
to understand	(听/看)懂	4
university	大学	4
unpleasant to listen to	难听	4
up, above	上	4
upstairs	楼上	6
vegetable; dish	菜	8
vehicle	车, 汽车	1, 6
venue	地点	8
very	很	6
visit, to visit	参观	5
to walk	走(路)	4
to want	要	8
warm	暖	2
water	水	4

weather	天气	4
weather forecast	天气预报	9
week	星期	4
welcome, to welcome	欢迎	5
west	西	6
the west	西方	
wind	风	4
wine	葡萄酒	5
to wish	祝	9
women's toilets	女厕所	5
wood; a surname	林	2
word	词	3
work, to work	工作	9
work unit	工作单位	8
worker	工人	4
to write	写	3
year	年	4
yellow	黄	7
yesterday	昨(天)	3, (9)
you (singular)	你	6
younger brother	弟弟	5
younger sister	妹妹	5
yuan (unit of Chinese currency)	元, 圆	8
zero	零	4

Other related titles

TEACH YOURSELF

CHINESE

Elizabeth Scurfield

Written for complete beginners, this book explains the complexities of spoken and written Modern Standard Chinese (otherwise known as Mandarin). Its logical and enthusiastic approach makes this notoriously difficult language straightforward and easy to learn.

Elizabeth Scurfield explains everything clearly along the way and gives you plenty of opportunities to practise what you have learnt. The graded structure means that you can work at your own pace, arranging your learning to suit your needs.

Teach Yourself Chinese has many unique features:

- You can decide whether or not to learn the script. If you don't need it, just follow the *pinyin* transcriptions
- The summary of key grammar allows you to look up difficult points in seconds
- The extensive two-way vocabulary lists mean that this truly is a complete course in one volume

By the end of this course you will be able to take a fully active part in the life and culture of China and Chinese-speaking people everywhere.